Lori's Lies and Family Ties

Healing from the Tylee and J.J. Tragedy

by

Rex Conner and Adam Cox

We dedicate this book first to the memory of the victims of this despicable evil, which has taken lives and irreparably scarred countless others, especially to Tylee and J.J.

We also dedicate it to the army of law enforcement, media, and people throughout the world who have been united in the cause of bringing the known and unknown conspirators of this evil to justice.

Finally, we dedicate this book for all the people who have given us support and to those family members and close friends who are still struggling with this daily devastation.

Acknowledgements

We must acknowledge Kay and Larry Woodcock for loving J.J. enough to get this cause started and for being the tireless face in the battle to find justice and of the outpouring of love that united us all.

Also, for us, Nate Eaton became the face of the army of media that has carried this story into all of our lives and hearts. Thank you to all.

We also acknowledge the tremendous assistance we received to produce this book from Jane Alvey Harris and her Many Realms Media team of brilliant editors. During Lori's trial we thanked, among others, Lori's defense team for the task they had to perform without much to work with from Lori. Similarly, any legible content in this book from which it's easy to extract the meaning of is because of the Many Realms Team working without well-developed input from us. Thank you!

Tylee Ryan & Joshua Jackson Vallow (JJ)

Sent to us by listener Karen Mazaham

COX FAMILY TREE

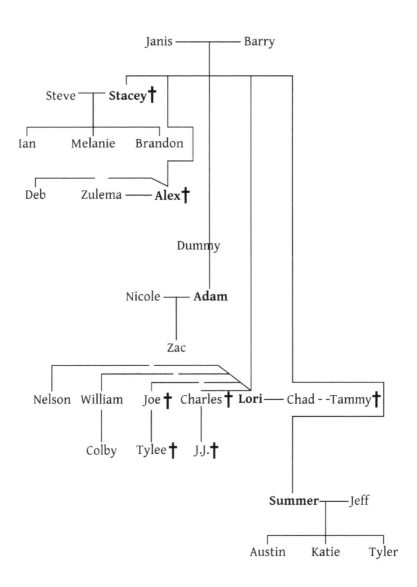

Contents

PREFACE:

"I am transitioning into an immortal being."

My sister, Lori Vallow Daybell, said those words to me as we stood in her kitchen one day.

I stood rooted to the floor, stunned. My thoughts spun as I tried to reconcile her words both with reality and with my life-long relationship with this person standing only a few feet away from me. My sister.

Lori leaned back against the counter, arms folded loosely across her chest, head held high and confident. The light streaming in through the window behind her caught in her long blonde hair, making it shine like gold.

Was she joking?

Narrowing my eyes, I studied her face. Nothing in the cast of her gaze or the lines of her mouth suggested anything but absolute seriousness.

Who is this person? My mind reeled. This isn't the girl I grew up with. This isn't the woman I knew. What has happened to my sister?

1

All the while she watched me, waiting for my response.

What would *you* say if your sister told you she was 'transitioning to an immortal being'?

A statement like that would probably catch you off guard, right? It certainly caught me off guard. My mind churned, presenting different options; none seemed right.

First, I considered changing topics, hoping to distract her away from her bizarre revelation with something mundane. But the set of her shoulders told me she wasn't going to be sidetracked.

Next, I thought about urging her to seek help, suggesting she go to therapy or talk to a church leader. I even briefly considered quoting scripture, but who was I kidding? I've never been the kind of guy who reads verses of scripture to someone – no matter the circumstance. Lori knew that as well as I did; she wouldn't listen to anything like that from me.

There has to be some way I can reason with her, my big-brother-mind told me. But hearing those words, that completely unhinged statement, so overwhelmed me that I could barely organize my thoughts, let alone debate her rationally.

Nothing I could think to say seemed equal in scope to the bewildering words she'd uttered, or to the conviction radiating from her posture.

Above all the swirling thoughts in my mind, one sat ready to leap from the tip of my tongue: *are you freaking nuts?!* I wanted to shout the words. But my tongue stuck to the roof of my mouth, unwilling – *unable* – to respond. I'd always been quick with a joke or a piece of advice, even in what I consider to be pretty serious circumstances. Not now. For the first time in my life, I had nothing to say.

About thirty seconds went by. Thirty seconds of silence while Lori studied my face and I leaned on the counter, studying hers, unable or unwilling to speak the words I knew would provoke her to anger. Thirty seconds that dragged like an eternity. With each second that slipped by, the pressure to say something only grew.

Thankfully – or maybe not? – Lori became impatient. "You think I'm crazy, don't you?" she asked, arms still folded across her chest, sun still creating a halo around her head.

"Yes!" I wanted to shout, but I stopped myself. Maybe my big-brother brain was still in charge, preventing me from arguing with my little sister. Still, it felt wrong to not say *anything*. What ended up coming out of my mouth was, "I don't think you're crazy, Lori. But what you're telling me isn't true."

Diplomatic enough, I reasoned, hoping that would be the end of it. I certainly wasn't going to encourage her or entertain her delusional beliefs. Lori knew me. She knew I wasn't interested in fringe religious ideology, even if that hadn't stopped her from saying what she said in the first place. My answer was straightforward, though, simple and non-combative. What more was there to say?

"I don't have to eat ever again," she said, ignoring my comment and deflating my hopes of an easy way out of this, her gaze locked on mine. "And if you shoot me, the bullet won't hurt me, Adam. My body has almost completed the process of becoming immortal."

The hair on the back of my neck stood straight up, my gut clenching tighter with every word coming out of her mouth.

"That's not true," I repeated, trying and failing to come up with a better response.

A kind of impatient disappointment twitched at the corner of my sister's mouth while she weighed and measured me with her eyes. Then, without saying another word, she turned on her heel and walked out of the kitchen without saying goodbye.

That brief, bizarre conversation I had with Lori in her kitchen, four years ago turned out to be the last time we spoke. When she turned her back and walked away from me was the moment Lori officially shut me out of her life.

Introduction

Adam

Tylee and J.J. were the best kids my sister could have asked for. I know I speak for my whole family when I say we are endlessly grateful to have had them in our lives. Tylee was a bright, vivacious, and funny girl. J.J. was a loving, rambunctious, very much loved little boy. My sister seemed like the perfect mother. She protected them. She cherished them. She raised them to love Christ. They were a close family who stuck together – no matter what hardships befell them.

On June 9th, 2020, investigators combed the backyard of a quiet home in Rexburg, Idaho. Buried in the backyard of a man I've never met, they found the body of a young boy, wrapped in duct-tape, curled up in a trash bag. The body was confirmed hours later to belong to J.J.

Tylee's remains were buried a few meters away and had to be identified using dental records. She was 16 at the time. J.J. was only seven.

In 2023, my sister was found guilty of their murder.

A full accounting of the events that lead to a small army of officers, deputies, and FBI agents scouring the Idaho home is beyond the scope of this book. A timeline in the appendix is available for a more detailed overview of the case, but even that has been simplified. In spite of how ridiculous and melodramatic all of this sounds, what I'm about to tell you is only a fraction of the whole story.

We begin in a crowded conference center in St. George, Utah. It's October 2018, and hundreds of Christians have gathered to talk about a foreboding topic: the end of the world.

This group calls themselves Preparing a People. Throughout the day, a handful of speakers take to the stage to discuss the imminent Second Coming of Christ, and how to prepare for it.

Among the speakers is Chad Daybell, a self-published author of dozens of books. He tells an enraptured audience that the apocalypse is beginning soon, and cites living conditions in North Korea, hurricane Irma, an earthquake in Mexico, and fires in Montana as evidence. Then, he likens himself to conspiracy theorist

Charlie Frost, from the movie *2012*, who predicted the end of the world – and who no one believed until it was too late.

My sister Lori was in the audience. She'd read Chad's books and had been a fan for a while. She met Chad after his speech at the conference book signing. As he sold and signed books and met with attendees, she walked up to him, introduced herself, and promised not to leave his side until he'd sold every single book he'd brought with him. At the end of that day, he professed to her that the two of them had, in fact, been married many times in past lives.

That was the start of their bizarre and adulterous relationship. Both Chad and Lori were married to other people when they met. Lori's husband at the time, Charles Vallow, was her third. Although he and Lori never had children together, Charles was an excellent father to his own sons from a previous marriage, to Lori's son and daughter from her previous marriages, and to their adopted son, J.J. Vallow.

Chad, on the other hand, was married to his first wife, Tammy. At the time he claimed to be 'spiritually betrothed' to my little sister, Chad and Tammy had been married for 29 years.

Both Charles and Tammy died the following year. Charles was shot by my brother Alex on July 11, 2019. Tammy passed in her sleep on October 19, 2019. It was later determined that she had not died of natural causes, as was initially recorded, but was murdered.

On November 5, 2019, only thirteen days after Tammy was buried, Lori and Chad were married. In their wedding photos, the newly widowed lovers danced and laughed on a sandy beach in

Kauai, dressed in white and wearing leis. No family members from either side were present. Not even their kids. In fact, none of either of their family members knew anything about the marriage.

After they met at the conference, Chad and Lori began exchanging texts and emails. The messages paint a picture of a delusional, religious fairy tale the two were convinced they were living in. Chad and Lori were the main characters – a pair of pure souls destined for one another, sent on a mission from God to protect the true believers of the world, and vanquish the forces of evil who stood in their way.

The people in their lives at the time, namely their family members, ended up being unwilling cast members in a gruesome tragedy. Chad claimed to have the ability to discern light spirits from dark spirits with mathematical precision. In one email to Lori, he presented a list of her family members. Each name was accompanied by a number and letter, denoting how dark or light he claimed each spirit to be. Both Tylee and J.J.'s names were written on that list. Tylee was listed as dark.

In other emails and texts, Chad and Lori talked about zombies – someone whose light spirit had been forcefully usurped by a dark one. During the process of usurpation, the evil spirit invades, claiming the body as its host, and casting the original spirit into a limbo state. The only way to free the original spirit from limbo was to kill the body and its new host.

Lori and Chad had fully developed these beliefs by the time Lori approached me in her kitchen and told me she was transitioning from a mortal to an immortal being.

Of course, back then, I didn't know anything about the light/dark scale. I had no idea that conversation would be our last, nor that the occasion would mark the last time Lori and I would be in the same room together.

The things Lori shared with me in the kitchen that morning alarmed me, but they weren't the first unusual or upsetting things she'd ever said to me. It wasn't even the first time I had been concerned enough as an older brother to raise the alarm to my family that something was wrong.

Previously, Lori had confided in me that she'd seen Jesus Christ face to face, and that he was "a beautiful man." She told me she'd seen Satan's face as well, and he was "even more beautiful than the Son of God."

Plenty of people have accused me of "letting" the events that followed happen. They argue that if I'd done more, spoken louder, *made* Lori see reason, I could have prevented the deaths of Charles, Tylee, J.J., Tammy, and Alex. Many people blame me for what happened.

Those are pretty harsh accusations. They've kept me awake for many, seemingly endless, ink-black nights. I've grappled with demons in my own head telling me that I should have done more. I've heard everything from, *"How did he not see it coming?"* to

"Why didn't he go to the police?" and *"Why didn't he have her committed?"*

I've asked myself thousands of times over years of sleepless nights if there was something more I could have done to stop Lori from conspiring to commit and committing crimes that ripped our family apart and devastates everyone who hears about it.

Despite my penchant for self-blame, in this case I have finally come to the firm conclusion that my answer is no. No. There wasn't anything I could have done to stop her. I *did* try to intervene several times and in several ways.

It is not my intention in writing this book to clear my name from aspersions of guilt. People will think what they want no matter what I say. My first intention for writing this book is to reveal the history of Lori's lies, and to identify the behaviors and patterns that led her to stray so far from the path she set out on as a little girl growing up in our family. I also want to bear witness to the disastrous impact her lies have had on her family. My second intention is to document our quest to process and come to grips with everything that has happened. In processing, I seek to heal, and to share the insights I gain with as many people as I can who were and are affected by these events.

PART ONE: Family Ties

CHAPTER ONE: Meet the Coxes

Adam

By now, you know who I am, but I'll introduce myself anyway – for politeness' sake. I'm Adam Cox, the brother of Lori Vallow Daybell and Alex Cox. Tylee and J.J., two of the victims, are my niece and nephew, but we'll get to that a little later. You'll also hear from my uncle Rex throughout the book, but for now, we have other introductions to make.

I'm the third of five children born to Janis Lee Cox and Barry Lynn Cox. My siblings are Stacey Lynne Cox (1966 - 1988), Alexander Lamar Cox-Pastenes (1968 -2019), Lori Norene Cox (born June 26, 1973), and Summer Novelle Cox (1975). I was born in 1969, a year after Alex.

We were a big, close, happy family, and we've always loved spending time together. Growing up, we played games, watched movies, and enjoyed each other's company. My dad was a huge advocate for having a good work ethic. He grew up working hard because his dad instilled that value in him. Every Saturday morning, he'd wake us up at 7:00 A.M. for a big family breakfast of his homemade pancakes, eggs, sausage, and bacon. After breakfast, my dad, Alex, and I went outside and did all the yard work. This included everything from cleaning the pool, the front yard, the backyard, the side yard, the trash area, the garage, the driveway, and even the roof.

While we were busy outside, my mom, along with Stacey, Lori, and Summer, cleaned the house and did laundry. As we worked, we'd blast our music, taking turns as to who got to pick which music we listened to. Alex liked rock and classic rock, so we took our boombox outside and cranked it up. Stacey loved 80s music – though, of course, back then it was called new music – so she would crank up the stereo in her room and blast Duran Duran, Rick Springfield, the Go Go's, and more. As a family we worked from 7:00 A.M. to about 4:00 P.M. with a quick lunch break which was usually someone making a Del Taco run.

We also watched football as a family. My mom would get everyone's picks of who would win that week. If your picks won the most games that week, you'd get a six-pack of your favorite soda all to yourself. I really didn't like soda, so I'd ask for a six-pack of chocolate pudding when I was the champion of the week. Unfortunately – and completely unfairly, if you ask me – chocolate pudding only came in four-packs back then, so I was always cheated out of a whole third of my prize. But at least I had bragging rights. When anyone won, they'd spend the whole next week bragging to the rest of us.

We've always been a competitive family. We all liked to win in the various games and competitions we had. Also, we loved to color. We bought crayons and markers and colored pencils and tons of coloring books. We'd spend hours trying to color the perfect pictures, partially to earn bragging rights about whose was the best.

Singing was a competition between Lori and Summer, who both have great singing voices, whereas Alex, Stacey, and I decidedly did *not*. Lori and Summer were also dancers and spent hours choreographing dance routines to different songs to perform in mini talent shows for us, as well as for friends, and relatives whenever they'd visit or we'd visit them.

Every week after church on Sunday, we would come home and eat a big Sunday dinner. It was a staple in our family. Because our church meetings ended around noon, we'd usually eat supper at 1:00 P.M. Everybody helped with cooking and setting the table. Some of my favorite Sunday meals were homemade tacos and roast with mashed potatoes.

My childhood was a happy one. I believe my siblings would say the same. We had a lot of fun and laughed a lot. Alex had a real knack for doing impressions of people. He could meet a stranger, and in minutes be able to mimic their facial expressions, body language, and voice. He especially loved doing impressions of my dad and kept us in stitches. We all had fun laughing at ourselves and with each other, including Lori.

Despite Lori being five years younger, she and I were closer in a lot of ways than some of our other siblings. We got along really well and had similar interests and a similar sense of humor. I have some really good memories of us playing together outside, throwing the football around with her and Summer.

Our shared bond meant I got to see her doing what she loved as we grew up. Things like singing, dancing, and roller-skating. She liked to set her stereo speaker out of the window of her room so she could roller skate to her favorite songs in the front yard.

One thing Lori and I had in common was looks. We both went through a chubby phase as pre-teens. The teasing at school was tough, but it helped that she and I could bond with each other as we tried to figure out how to deal with it.

She and I also both hated scary movies. Even though they tried, the rest of our family couldn't talk us into watching them. Neither of us liked being left home alone, either. We'd scare ourselves silly with stories of ghosts, boogey-men in the basement, and monsters in the closet.

By the time we were teens and had gone through puberty, Lori and I had each transformed from pudgy, ugly ducklings to athletic extroverts, though we still avoided scary movies.

Some of the fears and anxieties we shared were less paranormal. While my family was pretty good at keeping up with appearances, we had our fair share of problems. For instance, we always lived in a nice house in a nice neighborhood, and my dad drove a nice car, but there were times when money was really tight.

So tight, that we kids went to school without lunch money on more occasions than I like to remember. I'd duck out of the cafeteria and hide out in the locker room so no one would know I didn't have anything to eat.

I know these things weighed heavy on Lori's mind, too. Sometimes we'd talk about the things that scared us, and sometimes we didn't. One thing I do know is that Lori's testimony in our church gave her great comfort. When she was feeling most anxious, she would use the power of prayer as a comfort.

All five of the Cox siblings were born and raised as members of the Church of Jesus Christ of Latter-Day Saints.

This isn't a book about religion, but it is, in part, a book about Lori, and her religion has always played a central role in her life. In light of this, Rex and I have decided that it's necessary to provide some information about our shared family's beliefs, if only to show how corrupted and twisted Lori's beliefs became later in her life.

If you aren't familiar with the beliefs of the Latter-Day Saints, I invite you to read our Thirteen Articles of Faith, which are a very brief description of the tenets that stand as the cornerstone of our religion. To summarize, we believe in the Godhead, like all other Christian religions, though we believe that God the Father; His son, Jesus Christ; and the Holy Ghost are three separate and individual beings. We believe that the Latter-Day Saint church is led by a living, modern-day prophet, currently Russell M. Nelson, the 17th man to serve as prophet, seer, and revelator of the church. Another thing that distinguishes us from other Christian faiths is that we believe every righteous member of the church is entitled to both a personal relationship with our Lord and Savior, Jesus Christ, and personal revelation through the gift of the Holy Ghost, who is given as a comforter and guide when each member is confirmed after their baptism at age eight (or later).

My parents are both converts to the church. My dad joined at the age of 19 and served a mission to the U.K., while my mom was baptized at the age of nine.

My siblings and I were all 'born under the covenant,' meaning that our parents had been sealed for Time and All Eternity – as members of the Church of Jesus Christ of Latter-day Saints would say it – in the temple when they were married. Temples are especially sacred in our religion, considered separate from our regular churches.

Adult members of the Church who are faithful and follow the gospel are able to apply for and receive a special recommend allowing them to attend the temple and do sacred work there. There are currently 315 Latter-day Saint temples throughout the world, as of September 2023, and construction of 20 new temples have been announced.

Because my parents were interviewed and found worthy of temple recommends, they were able to be sealed in the temple. This is a very special privilege and comes with special covenants and special blessings. One of the blessings promised to my parents when they were sealed in the temple was that their family would be eternal, meaning that we would still be a family in the next life after our deaths in this life. Growing up, our parents often shared with us their testimonies of eternal families and truthfulness of the restored gospel of the Church of Jesus Christ of Latter-Day Saints.

The Coxes were always devout church members. My mom made sure we went to church every Sunday. Even when I was a teenager, playing pretty much every sport there was and growing like a weed, and I'd beg her to, *"Please let me stay home and sleep-in just this once!"* The answer was always a resounding NO. The Coxes went to church, no ifs, ands, or buts.

We participated in youth activities and served in various callings (volunteer positions within the church). We all played church sports, and my mom even coached the church's softball team for a few years. When I was ten years old, I vividly remember helping my mom coach the girls on her softball team, who were aged 12 to-17. Lori, who was on the team, made it clear she didn't want special treatment just because her mom was the coach. Mom had me demonstrate how to pitch, hit, and field balls, and then practice with them. Mom led her team to the state championship year after year.

Our family read the Bible and Book of Mormon, as well as other Church scripture, and listened to talks from church authorities at home, in weekly church meetings, and in after-school activities. As a family, the Coxes lived the scripture from the Book of Mormon that reads, "Adam fell that men might be, and men are that they might have joy." (2 Nephi 2:25) In other words, we applied the teachings of the restored gospel to our daily lives and tried to emulate Christ's teachings and examples. Our parents taught us to live Christ-centered lives every day, not in preparation for the end of times, but as a testament to His sacrifice, and to be good Christians.

As I've mentioned before, Lori's faith and testimony were very important to her growing up, and as an adult. One anecdote that demonstrates her mindset took place shortly after Lori turned eight and was baptized and confirmed a member of the church.

Lori and Summer were playing in the front yard one day. Like all sisters do sometimes, they got into an argument over something. I don't remember what it was about, but I do remember hearing Lori say to Summer, "If you want to hit me, then do it. I will just turn the other cheek like Jesus said to do."

Well, Summer, who was six at the time, took Lori at her word. She slapped Lori right across the cheek. I can still hear that *smack!*

Lori stood there with tears in her eyes, dumbfounded, her cheek bright red.

But then, slowly, Lori turned her face to the other side and said, "I'm not going to hit you back. Jesus said to turn the other cheek. If you want to hit me again, then go ahead."

I was too stunned to do anything except watch as Summer took her up on the offer.

At that point, Lori broke into sobs and high-tailed it back to the house with two red cheeks.

I'm not sure what Lori learned from that experience, but I do know that she took the Savior's words very seriously.

CHAPTER TWO: Hindsight

Adam

The things I've shared about our family dynamics, my bond with Lori, and our family's beliefs as members of the Church of Jesus Christ of Latter-day Saints are as honest and accurate a summary as I can make them in this short space. And yet, the public insists that I and my family members attempt to pick apart experiences and conversations and family vacations so that we can precisely categorize the different parts of Lori's identity. The demand to know if Lori was always the way she is now. Was she always a liar? Was she always crazy? Was she always hyper-religious?

Lori's faith was no different from the rest of us growing up. At least not so radically that any of us noticed. She never claimed to be a god, nor to have the ability to predict the future, nor the possession of immortality. She was a faithful member of the church like we all were. Her testimony in the gospel and of eternal families was a source of comfort to her in times of anxiety, as I've previously mentioned. And, I believe her desire for an eternal family of her own prompted her to be rash in her decisions to rush into her first two marriages, at least. But her religious beliefs didn't become extreme until decades later.

As far as answering whether or not she was always a liar, or if she was always crazy, my honest answer is no. She never exhibited any behaviors growing up in our house as my little sister that would ever have led me to imagine – not in my very worst nightmares – that she could ever be capable of the things she's done.

Some people will still insist that what I've shared of our childhood can't be the whole story, that there must be ugly secrets I'm refusing to talk about, given how Lori ended up. But I grew up in the same family, and I haven't gone on to murder anyone.

Before you read any further, it's important for me to make it clear that neither Rex nor I are psychologists. Neither of us have training in developmental sciences or anything like that. At the same time, most of you reading this probably don't either. Yet, don't you all have insight to share about your families, about your time growing up, about how that might have shaped you? All that's to say, take this with a grain of salt. The insights we offer are as men, fathers, and family members; hopefully there's something helpful to discover as we comb through it all.

Human beings, our personalities and beliefs are complicated. I believe the different ways each of us contemplates life, reacts under stress, and approaches the unknown spring from aspects that are equal parts nurture and nature. Of course, the environment in which a person is raised influences their development. How could it not?

Lori, Alex, and I all grew up in a shared environment. We all received the same type of nurture, for the most part. But from where I sit now, after everything that's happened, it is apparent that our natures couldn't be more different.

Every family has some level of dysfunction. If you're reading this and saying, "Not my family!" then you might need to take a closer look. But then again, not all dysfunction is the same. When humans – with all their differences in personality, perspective, and history – interact with one another, some level of discord is unavoidable. But when one or more members of a group *willfully* act in a way that's harmful to the others?

That's different.

Later in her life, Lori's actions would create dysfunction on that second, more serious level. As I've recounted above, our family had what I believe to be a fairly normal level of dysfunction.

So, if she wasn't born crazy and a liar, and she wasn't a crazy liar growing up, when did it all start? When did Lori start down the path that led her to conspire with our brother Alex and her lover Chad Daybell to commit the murders of her husband, two of her children, and her lover's wife?

Personally, with hindsight, I believe it started decades later when she became involved with preppers, which we'll discuss later in our story.

But well before then, right around the time she was a senior in high school, Lori's attitude and behavior changed. I believe that, from the perspective of where we are now, we can look back and recognize the beginnings of a mindset that led to behaviors that later became habits, and which over time allowed her to separate further and further from her conscience. Rex, who is an expert in the field of human performance, will discuss what this process might look like in the next chapter.

For my part, I'll pick up with where I left off.

I mentioned before in the section about the common bonds Lori and I shared: that we had both been on the heavy side as kids, but that we both thinned out after going through puberty. In high school, Lori became a cheerleader and grew quite popular.

I'd moved out at that point, but when she called to tell me she'd made the cheerleading squad, I was happy for her. I was less happy when I found out she'd started dating Nelson Yanes.

Nelson lived in our neighborhood. His brother Robert was in my older sister Stacey's class. I never had any communication with either of them growing up. Nelson was in Lori's grade, and the two of them started dating in high school. I was out of the house by that time, so I didn't get to watch them interacting firsthand, but I knew who he was, and I knew he didn't have a good reputation.

I have no idea why Lori was attracted to Nelson. He was a shorter, super skinny, non-athletic drug dealer. Lori was a popular cheerleader with a lot of guys giving her attention. From what I heard, the only thing Nelson had was maybe a bit of charm; he was a confident smooth talker. I really only had a few encounters with Nelson, but he came across as someone who knew how to influence others.

Our parents taught us that the company you hang out with says something about you, but Lori didn't seem to care what people thought about her hanging out with Nelson. She was possibly too busy enjoying the drugs Nelson supplied her with. I don't know how long she took drugs – it could have been for a week or a year.

My parents were both alarmed and concerned when Lori announced she was moving out and moving in with Nelson. They were even more upset when they found out she planned to marry him. Our entire family felt that way. My dad forbade her from eloping and tried to force her to move home. I guess he hadn't learned yet that, as an adult over the age of 18, Lori had decided no one could make her do anything. And boy was she going to show us that.

Probably with just that in mind, she went to the police and got a restraining order against every member of our family.

Then, she eloped with Nelson Yanes.

Afterward, Lori never confided in me about what made her decide to have her marriage with Nelson annulled, but I know her well enough to make some educated guesses. As I mentioned before, one of Lori's goals had always been to have a big, happy, eternal family – a happy, *church-attending* family, specifically. She might not have been living all the commandments, like "honor thine father and mother," but her determination to have an eternal family never wavered.

So, my guess is that she realized Nelson wasn't it. He wasn't someone who could be her partner in creating that picture-perfect family in her mind. Lori thought that as soon as they got married, the drugs and partying would stop and Nelson would suddenly grow up and become a respectful family man. She thought that, with her guidance and love, he would want the same things, and that he'd give up dealing and using drugs and become an active church member.

This belief that she could bring out the best in people and save them from themselves is something we'll see repeated throughout Lori's story.

I'm guessing that being married to someone with no job or future was the turning point. Or, maybe it was as simple an explanation as realizing she'd made a huge mistake.

Whatever Lori's motivation, our family forgave her for the restraining order and for her rash, juvenile decisions. When enough time had passed, we were able to joke about it as we addressed it. She'd been 18 years old. Everyone makes mistakes when they're 18 years old.

CHAPTER THREE: Natural Law

Rex

As Adam mentioned, I have some experience with human behavior, having worked in the field of human performance for the past several decades and earned several educational degrees that inform my work, including two master's degrees and a doctorate.

Adam and I have known and loved Lori since the day she was born. However, neither of us have spent any time inside her mind or heart. We can't perfectly pinpoint the moment she made the decision that led her to such a dark place. We *can* share what we recognized along the way. We can also speculate with you, the reader, as to how and why she chose to follow such an evil, tragic path.

Without knowing the actual beginning of the sequence, the first visible decision that triggered everything was her first marriage with that man – who was actually a boy – named Nelson. Like Adam said, the rest of the family wasn't happy. Lori's parents adamantly opposed the marriage, but Lori had already decided to go ahead with it. It lasted only weeks. That's how long it took Lori to admit it was a mistake, get out of it, and return home.

Lori's decision-making process works the same way it does for all of us. We all build habits to make the majority of decisions we face every day – the big decisions and the small ones. We have to use habits; some say we make more than 30,000 decisions per day during our waking hours. Doing the math, we are awake somewhere around 60,000 seconds each day. There's simply no way we could go through a conscious decision-making process every two seconds of our waking life. Think about the many decisions you make by habits you have developed over your lifetime – it's probably too many to list.

Ask yourself: how did you develop most of those habits, especially in your early years? The answer for all of us is that most of them were developed unconsciously. For example, think of your eating habits. In my case, I did not consciously decide how and what to eat when I was a child. I mostly ate when I could and avoided foods I didn't like. Later in life, when I finally admitted that most of my eating habits weren't getting me the health results I wanted, I found it quite painful to try and change them.

Like with food, most of the habits we have developed unconsciously were guided by our appetites, our egos, our impulses, and our passions. That is not healthy, conscious decision-making.

Many of us believe there are sources outside of us that try to influence us toward good or evil. But those same appetites, egos, impulses, and passions are not external sources. They are just a natural part of our experience in life. They aren't inherently "good" or "bad" – in fact, they can add a lot of good to our lives through self-preservation, spontaneity, excitement, and happiness. But they can also *become* bad if we're not deliberate. Appetites naturally want to be continually fed, and to eventually control us. Thankfully, these internal appetites, impulses, and passions are held in check by another very natural part of us.

We each have an internal guidance system that observes and recognizes natural law while warning us of potential consequences. It doesn't get caught up in our emotions or in our values.

In the case of Lori's first marriage, it's likely that her internal guidance system told her something like, "If you marry Nelson, you will:

- Alienate your parents.
- Feel independence being away from your family.
- Have financial hardships.
- Live in the toxic environment he and his friends create."

The other part of Lori's natural internal influences – the fear, ego, appetites, and limited reasoning – might have countered with, "If you marry him, you will:

- Not miss out on a much more fun environment.
- Show your parents just who is in charge of your life.
- Be able to enjoy sex, drugs, and alcohol without guilt.
- Be an adult, making adult decisions."

And so it goes for all of us. It is a natural part of life. Of course, the pressures, emotions, and complexities increase when the external sources of good and evil weigh-in, tipping the scales.

In the long run, natural laws prevail.

But what are natural laws, exactly?

It's commonly understood that we can make or control our own decisions, but we can't control other people, or the consequences of the decisions we make. Consequences are controlled by the laws of nature, or natural laws.

In fact, natural laws control the entirety of our existence on this planet.

Gravity is an example of a natural law. It stays in control no matter *who* you are, no matter *where* you are, and no matter *when* you are there. It is not emotional, and it does not make exceptions.

How often do you think about the natural laws that govern every aspect of your life – every aspect of your existence? Most of us rarely give it a conscious thought. Strange, isn't it? To ignore the laws that govern our daily existence?

Maybe the reason we don't think about these laws is because not all of them are as apparent as gravity is. This stands to reason, as most of the rest of the natural laws in our lives – though equally ever-present – don't have quite as obvious consequences and names. Some of them don't even have colloquial names.

Science does put a name on some of them, however. Like momentum, for example, or cause and effect and perpetual motion. And there are natural laws that often get grouped together, like the laws of thermodynamics, motion, and the concept of rhythm. These laws are mostly studied by professionals in subject-specific related fields. These laws are predictable, quantifiable, and are able to be expressed as equations.

In contrast there is very little energy spent by individuals to identify, interpret, and define the equally important – albeit unquantifiable and intangible – natural laws that impact and govern our daily lives, such as trust, motivation, human performance, self-preservation, or moral standards.

However, as much as we often neglect to do so, we *can* recognize intangible natural laws, and especially the *violations* of natural laws, in our daily lives.

Consider these examples:

When someone drives drunk, we can see the increased likelihood of impaired reactions resulting in injury.

When people engage in angry confrontations, we can see the likelihood of damaged relationships.

When we witness someone experience extreme emotional pain, we can predict their likely reaction of escaping to their coping strategy of choice to deal with it.

We can also recognize these types of consequences in ourselves when we are not blinded to them by our natural traits of FEAR: Fear, Ego, Appetites, and/or Reasoning.

Recognizing intangible natural laws and their consequences is what we call "common sense." We aren't necessarily thinking in terms of natural laws when we use our common sense, but only because it's so ingrained in our being, like any other 'sense' we might have. It's common because everyone has it, even if we don't use it all the time.

To leap ahead in Lori Vallow's story, she had decided long before she and Chad murdered her children and hid their bodies in Chad's pet cemetery that she was through with following her common sense; it wasn't providing what she wanted out of life. She had already replaced common sense with a fantasy that she and Chad created together as a result of their combined fears, egos, appetites, and limited, perverse reasoning.

That didn't happen suddenly. It was a path of countless decisions in which Lori consciously allowed the natural side of herself to overrule her common sense. Appetites and ego want to control us. The only times they don't is when we consciously allow our common sense to limit them. Like I said at the beginning of this discussion, we all use that same decision-making process, and we all have the same natures. Lori chose to allow her natural self to go unchecked.

Now, this can also account for the external forces that many of us believe are trying to influence us. We have many names for them: good and evil, virtue and vice, God and Satan, light and dark – the list goes on. The important thing is, the fact that these influences are external means we are each ultimately responsible for the decisions that we make. None of us – including Lori, Chad, and Alex – can claim that the "Devil made us do it," or that we just snapped, or that mental illness caused it.

There are many influences at play in each of our lives, both good and bad. Natural law dictates that we are each still responsible for our own decisions and actions. So, whatever might have influenced Lori to do what she did serves as no excuse.

She's still on the hook for everything.

I have more thoughts to share about this topic – about the way our minds function and the ways in which that might relate to Lori's actions. For now, I'll let Adam continue tracing Lori's path to marrying Chad Daybell and conspiring to commit multiple egregious crimes. I'll pop back in every once in a while to continue teasing out this thread.

CHAPTER FOUR: Identifying Patterns - Marriages Two through Four

Adam

Beyond offering some insight into how Lori interacted with her own conscience, examining Lori's next two marriages offers insight into a huge motivator in her life: her desire for a worthy partner with whom she could create an eternal family.

In the texts, emails, and phone calls we later discovered between Chad and Lori, they addressed each other like soul mates, before she was separated from her fourth husband, Charles Vallow. From the documented email and text messages shared in court during her trial, it was clear that in Chad, Lori believed she had finally found a religious and spiritual equal. Like a pair of like-minded engineers or scientists, spoke endlessly to each other about their beliefs.

That was never the case with the four husbands she'd had before, though, as much as she might have been searching for that level of connection in a partner.

And search she did. Life went on after Lori divorced Nelson, and we grew up. I moved to Austin, Texas, to become a radio personality, a career I would end up pursuing for the next thirty years.

To my surprise, Lori followed me there, not long after she and Nelson got their marriage annulled and asked if she could move in with me. She wasn't interested in living at home anymore. Her plan was to go to cosmetology to become a hairstylist.

This was in the early 90s, and I had a two-bedroom apartment in the bad part of town. The rent was cheap, but I'd just started my career. I told Lori that she could stay, but she'd need to buy her own groceries and pay for any other expenses she had. I wasn't in a position to support my little sister financially.

Lori ended up getting a job at The Chess King in the Barton Creek mall, and she started attending cosmetology school. I loved having her live with me. We got along great, but we were both busy and didn't see each other during the week. On the weekends, she'd tag along with me and some of my friends going out to clubs. Lori was charismatic and fun, and all my friends had crushes on her. She was nice to all of them but didn't have any interest in dating any of them.

Soon after getting her job at The Chess King, Lori became involved with one of her co-workers, William LaGioia. He told her some down-on-his-luck story about not having any place to live, and Lori took pity on him.

One day after work I was at home in my apartment unwinding when the front door opened and Lori and some guy I'd never met walked in.

"This is Will," Lori said. "He's my boyfriend."

I hadn't even known she was dating anyone.

"He's going to live with me in my room," she continued.

"He's going to do what?" I asked.

"No worries, man. I'll get groceries," Will said, offering to shake hands.

Maybe he thought a handshake would make Lori's announcement okay.

It didn't.

First off, Lori wasn't paying me rent, so her calling it 'her room' was a bit of a stretch.

Second, my first impression of Will – to put it bluntly – was that he was a loser. Will was about 6'2" and had slicked back black hair. He had the body of someone who worked out, but he talked like he didn't have much going on upstairs. Something about him rubbed me the wrong way from the get-go. The way he looked at Lori, the way that he was letting her do all the talking, the way he presented all the bad things that had happened to him like he didn't take any responsibility and the world was out to get him.

I didn't get it. Lori wasn't a loser. She had a lot going for her: looks, charm, intelligence, opportunity, talent, and support. I couldn't figure out what made her keep choosing losers. First

Nelson, and now this guy? She barely even knew this guy. She'd met him what, two weeks before?

I pulled Lori to the side and simply said, "He is *not* living here."

Lori blinked at me in surprise but recovered quickly. Her mouth drew into a thin, straight line. "Okay," was all she said. Then to Will she said, "Come on, we're leaving."

And that was that. Lori took her stuff, scraped together money from who knows where, and moved into her own apartment with Will. It had been about a year since she'd had her marriage to Nelson annulled.

Come to find out, I'd been right about him. From conversations with Lori, I discovered that Will was an opportunist and a victim. For instance, he hadn't graduated from high school (not his fault). He'd been arrested for fighting (not his fault). He'd been fired from his job (not his fault).

Will could get jobs, but he couldn't keep them very long. Lori was working and going to school. These two things meant that they were broke. I found out later that at one point while they were dating, Will got a job as a male stripper. His hours weren't regular, and he didn't have his own car, so he convinced Lori he needed her Honda CRX that my dad had bought for her. He'd say he was using it to drive to the strip club and to look for better jobs, but he'd really just drop her off at work and then cruise around in her car all day listening to loud music and picking up girls.

Lori and Will lived together off and on for four years before they got married on October 22, 1995. They fought a lot, and Lori would tell me later that he was verbally and physically abusive with her. Some of their fights were over the types of things you'd expect from a broke, young couple. But a lot of them revolved around something Lori carried with her from childhood: her devout faith.

Even though Lori was breaking commandments of the church right and left, she had a very strong testimony of the gospel and desperately wanted Will to become a member of the church. He would sometimes pretend to be interested for Lori's sake, but he didn't change the behaviors that Lori thought he should, and he didn't take any steps to be baptized. So, their fighting became worse.

And then Lori became pregnant.

Under these stressful circumstances, things inevitably took a turn for the worse.

Late one night, Lori called me from a station.

"Can you come get me?" she asked, her voice full of tears. "Will beat me up. He took my keys."

I can still see that night so clearly in my mind. I pulled into the gas station. Lori stood outside on the curb in a tight blue dress that emphasized her pregnant belly. Her left eye was swollen shut, already a dark shade of bruise-purple. Half her lip was twice as big as the other. Yet she stood there waiting for me with her head up, not cowering or hiding.

My heart lurched at the sight of her. Anger coursed through me. Anger at Will and sorrow for my little sister. I knew why she hadn't left him yet. She was a fighter, and she was pregnant. She wanted to make things work. She wanted a happy family.

"You know you have to leave him, right?" I asked, after we'd driven in silence for several minutes back to my apartment.

"Yes."

I was so relieved. We talked about a lot of things that night. About how things might not be easy for a while, but that she had the support of her family. What was important was that she wouldn't be living with her abuser anymore.

But it didn't last. Lori gave birth to her first child, Colby, on April 8, 1996. According to a criminal complaint she later filed against him, Will contacted her in July of that same year and begged her to come to Bracketville, Texas, where he was living with his parents, and attend his baptism into the Church of Jesus Christ of Latter-day Saints.

Will told Lori that their separation had inspired him to change his ways. He couldn't lose her. He'd been to counseling; he'd repented of his sins. He'd taken the missionary discussions and accepted God into his life. He promised that if she would take him back, he would be a devoted husband and father, and that he would work and provide for Lori and their son so Lori could stay at home and raise Colby.

Lori said yes. She was 23 years old. Pretty much as soon as she moved in with Will's family, Lori started preaching the gospel to them. It wasn't long before her mother-in-law joined the church.

But spreading the gospel couldn't distract Lori from mountains of evidence that he hadn't changed at all. She took Colby and left him again one night while he was passed out drunk, driving to San Antonio to stay with our parents. She also went back again when Will begged her to return again, promising that this time, it would be different.

Of course, it wasn't. The last straw was when she found out that Will had gotten some other girl pregnant while she was at home raising their baby boy.

By the end of 1996, Lori faced the writing on the wall and asked for a divorce. Even after giving him all those second chances, she had to face the fact that he wasn't ever going to be her partner in creating a big, happy, righteous family. I only wish she'd realized sooner.

Lori left Will, but not before having to resolve one more issue: custody of Colby. Lori wanted to take him with her, and let's be honest, even the little we've discussed so far about Will doesn't paint him as someone who would have been eager to pay child support. It probably could have been a real nasty court fight, but Will came up with a compromise pretty quickly. He suggested that if Lori would give him her car, the Honda CRX that my dad bought her, he would sign over all parental rights over Colby without a fuss. Lori agreed, and a child's father traded a car for his son. I wish it surprised me more.

I'm sharing these things not to get anyone to feel sorry for her or excuse her behavior because she had it rough in some of her early relationships. I'm sharing to show that once again, she met a man, thought she saw his potential, married him, then left him when she realized he couldn't give her what she wanted.

Again, hindsight is 20/20. At the time, everyone grieved with her and supported her. She was unlucky in love. She was still young. She wouldn't be so rash next time. But after everything that has happened, looking back on her second marriage I see the beginning of a pattern.

Lori could have had her pick of pretty much any guy, as far as I could tell. But Lori liked a project. She liked the idea of rescuing men from themselves. I believe she saw herself as someone who could reform emotionally damaged men. I think she told herself that these men she fell for so fast just needed a good woman by their side. I believe she saw herself as one half of a power couple, and it was up to her to take a man and mold him into the perfect partner.

Husband #3: Joe Ryan

After her divorce from William LaGioia, Lori moved back to Austin, Texas, and found work as a stylist in a hair salon. In 2001, at age 28, Lori met 40-something Joseph Ryan. They were married after a very brief, whirlwind courtship.

For a time, Lori and Joe seemed genuinely happy. Joe adopted Colby as his son. Then, on September 24, 2002, Lori and Joy welcomed their daughter – my niece, Tylee Ashlyn Ryan (September 24, 2002 – c. September 9, 2019) – to the world.

Joe wasn't a member of the church when Lori started dating him, but just like her second husband, Will, Lori persuaded him to convert and be baptized as a member of the Church of Jesus Christ of Latter-day Saints.

Initially, it looked like Lori's dream was finally coming true. She was finally going to have an eternal family who would all go to church together and live happily ever after.

But after a while, Lori decided Joe didn't fit the bill.

According to her, they would fight over sex a lot. Apparently, Lori wanted it, and Joe didn't. After they returned from their honeymoon, Lori called our mom and complained that they'd only had sex once during the whole trip.

This came as news to me. They'd had a child together, and they'd certainly seemed to have chemistry early on in their relationship.

I didn't really spend a lot of time around Joe, but the times I did, I didn't really know what to think of him. He was just...*odd*. He wasn't very personable, and he didn't really seem comfortable being around our family. Which is fine, we can be boisterous and loud. He just didn't fit in. Whenever we had family get-togethers, he'd go off by himself.

Joe had some kind of consulting job and seemed to make good money, but I could never really figure out what he did. Every time we had a conversation about his job, the details just never made sense to me. He wore turtlenecks all the time, he was never very open about himself, and he was always on his computer.

Worse, though, Joe seemed to have a short temper when dealing with Colby.

Don't get me wrong. I'm sure being a stepdad has its challenges, but that wasn't enough to explain the aggression.

Based on my personal interactions with Joe, I never felt that he really loved Colby. I witnessed Joe making plenty of criticism of him, but never offering any approval. Joe yelled at Colby for small little things. He'd stand over him to intimidate him, and sometimes grab him way too roughly. So many times, I wanted to intervene, but I never did. I thought it wasn't my place. I never saw him hug Colby or say tell him he loved him.

By the time I found out that they were struggling in their marriage, I'd already started asking myself the same question I'd asked twice before: why does Lori keep picking these guys to marry?

So how did this one end?

Not at all well.

One day, Lori said she found pornography on Joe's computer. Child pornography. A while later, Lori claimed that Joe had been molesting both Colby and Tylee.

I'm still not one-hundred percent sure about these allegations, especially in light of the fact that we know Lori is very capable of lying to hurt people she had previously claimed to love. Colby corroborated Lori's story, but he would have been very young at the time. It's possible that he believed it happened because Lori told him it happened. There was certainly no love lost between Joe and Colby.

Lori and Joe's divorce was finalized in 2005.

Lori has told a lot of lies about a lot of people – we'll get to plenty of them throughout this book. Additionally, Joe was legally cleared of all charges related to abusing J.J. and Tylee. There were times when I felt in my gut that Lori might have been telling the truth in this case, but we simply know so little that it's hard to take her word even for something as serious as this type of allegation. Now, I doubt we'll ever know.

At the time, however, the Cox family believed her one hundred percent. Our older brother Alex believed her and was so furious that he tased Joe and threatened to kill him in 2007. Alex served 90 days in an Austin, Texas, prison.

Alex had always been protective of his family. No one was going to mess with any of us if he had anything to say about it. But this time was different. This time went too far.

As we'll see, Lori was able to use Alex's natural sense of family loyalty to manipulate him. Tasering Joe was not the last time that Alex would act with extreme violence in what he believed was the defense of his little sister.

Husband #4: Charles Vallow

Lori met Charles Vallow (August 17, 1956 - July 11, 2019) while still living in Austin. Charles was originally from Louisiana and had that southern accent and plenty of charisma to go with it. Charles was a man's man, athletic, outgoing, successful. He played baseball for McNeese in 1975-76. He'd been divorced; and had two boys, Zack and Cole, from his previous marriage.

43

When Lori and Charles just started dating, Nicole, my wife at the time, and I went on a double date with them to a steakhouse. Lori and Charles seemed to be really into each other. Charles kept complimenting Lori, saying how beautiful she was. He seemed like he was smitten. I was happy because for the first time, I saw a man treating my little sister right.

Don't get me wrong, Charles wasn't perfect. At the time they met, he probably drank too much, and he also really liked his pain pills. Still, he was in a completely different league compared to Lori's previous husbands. In personality and charm, at least, he was Lori's equal. It was the first time I didn't ask myself why Lori chose guys that weren't on her level.

Lori and Charles tied the knot in February of 2006. Like Will and Joe, Charles wasn't a member of the Church. Also like Will and Joe, Lori was the one who introduced him to the gospel, and he was baptized a member after they were married. Lori went to work helping him with his drinking and pill habit, as well.

While Lori and Charles never had any biological children of their own together, their family grew when they adopted J.J. in 2013.

J.J. was Charles' great-nephew, the son of his nephew Todd Woodcock. When J.J. was born on May 25, 2012, neither of his biological parents were in a position to care for him. Both were addicts, and they knew as well as anyone that he deserved a more stable home. Initially, J.J.'s grandparents, Kay and Larry Woodcock, cared for their tiny newborn grandson. Within a few months, however, it was decided that the preemie needed more care than his grandparents could provide. Charles and Lori welcomed J.J. into their home with open arms.

Rex

I'm jumping in here to share my memories and impressions of J.J.

Because of J.J.'s struggles in the womb of an addicted mother, his upper-body strength was well above average. He used that strength as you might expect a boy who also had exceptional energy would: he enjoyed dismantling anything he could get his hands on. He wasn't angry. He was just an exuberant little guy enjoying what he did.

Four-year-old J.J. required non-stop, eyes-on supervision, especially in a group setting. Lori was often the leader of social activities, leaving that responsibility to be fulfilled by Charles. On the few occasions I saw them all together in J.J.'s early years, Charles didn't get many chances to talk. He just exchanged quick quips as he would hurry by to keep up with J.J.

At home, the only place J.J. could be left unsupervised for up to two minutes was in his highchair while he was occupied with food or something else to keep his interest.

For anyone who visited, we saw Lori, Charles, and Tylee demonstrating remarkable patience and love for each other and for J.J. Since Lori became the "most hated woman in the world," as described by her defense attorney, many people reject the idea that she was a good Mom. I get that. All I will say is that I've never seen inside her heart or mind. But the handful of brief times that I've stayed with Lori or been with her during family events, she was loving and patient to her children. I've never heard otherwise from any other family member, including one of the nannies she had for J.J. and Tylee.

Adam

Lori finally had a happy, stable family of her own. Charles blew her previous marriages out of the water as far as I could tell. After they were married, most of our family gatherings moved from our mom and dad's place to Lori and Charles' place. Lori was an excellent host and liked to be in charge. None of the rest of us minded. They had a beautiful, spacious home, and everyone felt welcomed.

I personally loved spending time with Charles. We weren't just related through marriage, like had been the case with all of her previous husbands, we were legitimate friends. Charles was a great conversationalist and all-around fun guy. He was politically conservative, and loved to talk politics, always telling me his views on what was going on in the country. Charles thrived on spending time with his family and was great at grilling. I have so many great memories of hanging out in Lori's and Charles' backyard in Arizona by the pool, shooting the breeze with Charles while he grilled up a fat, juicy steak.

So, was this finally it? on her path to happily ever after? Charles was an excellent father, a loving husband.

I wish it had been enough for her.

PART TWO: Lori's Lies

CHAPTER FIVE: Identity, Influence, and Manipulation

Rex

There are several times in this book in which we will reference our total belief that Lori and any co-conspirators, both known and unknown, are completely responsible for the murderous actions they took. Nothing about their mental states, their backgrounds, their beliefs, their possible tragic experiences, or their upbringing justifies their decisions to murder any of their victims.

We will even go as far as to answer the most common question of this entire horrific tragedy, which is some variation of, "How could they go from living the life they were portraying to killing the children and the other victims?"

While the events associated with this tragedy are endlessly complex, the answer to this question is relatively simple: they actively ignored their consciences.

Since we might all have slightly different beliefs or understandings about what a conscience is, we need to establish a working definition before relating it to the murders. The following is our belief and understanding about conscience. You don't have to agree with us or adopt our perspective. However, for you to understand what you will read about how this continues to unfold, it will help if you at least know the context we use when discussing the term.

Each of us has an 'internal guidance system.' It's available to us for the many decisions we make in life. We're prone to recognizing it most when the fruits of a difficult decision pay off positively for us. We also recognize it when, having chosen not to follow that guidance, we come to regret a decision that disappointed us or others who are important to us.

There are many names used for that internal guidance system, such as:

- · Conscience
- · Intuition
- · Divine guidance
- · Instinct
- · Inspiration
- · Sixth sense
- · Our gut
- · Universal energy
- · Wisdom of the Universe

In this book, we will interchange the terms "internal guidance" and "conscience." When you read either of those terms, here is the context in which they are used.

Your conscience, or internal guidance is:

· A natural part of every human on Earth, whether or not they access it or are aware of it.

· Unlimited because it is your connection with whatever power in the universe that resulted in you experiencing this life. If you believe in any form of God, it's your connection with God. If you believe we are a product of Nature and its natural evolution, it's your connection with Nature. If not, it's your connection with the natural laws that control this life. It is not the same as reasoning, which is limited to our own experiences, emotions, and understanding.

·Aligned with natural law, not with how we wish the world was, nor with people's actions. It indicates what the natural results of those actions will be.

· A reminder that people, including you, will be themselves, not whatever else we wish they would be.

· Free of emotion, so it can remain unbiased when decision time comes.

· Free of ego, so it can remain unaffected by other people's opinions.

· The unselfish balancing force to your appetites, impulses, and habits.

· A flawless indicator and reminder of the consequence of the decisions you consider.

Your conscience is one of the two great, natural, internal forces that determine all of the decisions you make in this life. Those two forces seem designed to bring balance to our lives as we strive to both address our personal needs and collaborate as we figure out how to navigate this life of ours.

The second great, natural, internal force is the combination of our ego, our appetites, our impulses, our fears, our emotions, and our reasoning, all things that generally cause us to consider our own well-being as we make the countless decisions required by life.

Let's emphasize here that these two forces are natural parts of each of us and are both important to living and enjoying life. They are often characterized, in our society, as light and dark, good and evil, positive and negative. But doesn't the quality of our life result in striking a balance between these two natural occurrences? Don't we thrive when our needs are met so we can contribute to life while finding and pursuing our 'higher self'?

Of course, if we give in to one natural part over the other, we fall out of balance and might spend all of our life energy trying to recover.

The most common example of this is when we give in to an appetite, an impulse, or a fear and ignore that internal guidance system. We realistically call the excess indulgence 'bad,' as it ushers in the predictable sorrows of addictions, rational lies, irrational reasoning, and lives of quiet desperation as we search for meaning.

Similarly, isn't the opposite imbalance equally as unhealthy and unproductive? When we pursue a belief that our natural self is evil and try to restrain it with our puny power of reasoning, fear, and self-loathing without the benefit of guidance of our conscience, aren't the results predictably bad? At least that was the experience of Siddhartha Gautama when he left his life of extreme privilege in search of the enlightenment that he felt he was lacking.

He tried finding that enlightenment through extreme self-deprivation, which brought him near death more than once. He did not find enlightenment until his perseverance resulted in him discovering that the "the middle way" – the internal balance of his natural selves – was the correct path to enlightenment. Teaching the insights from his journey resulted in a massive following which continues to grow to this day. There are 488 million of his followers striving for the middle way and honoring him as The Buddha.

On the other end of that spectrum are Lori and her co-conspirators. It's not a stretch to speculate that there are precious few people on this Earth who would describe them as balanced. Whether it's using the extreme religious rhetoric they espoused to commit murder and other acts of evil, or their obvious lust for sex, money, and power to justify it, there might not be a more extreme or tragic example of imbalance.

While there are many, many external influences that played into the drama, the simple explanation of how each of the murderers could degenerate from the apparently normal lives they seemed to have been living to that depth of evil is that they each consistently ignored their conscience over an undetermined period of time through countless decisions to satisfy their imbalanced, gluttonous cravings for sex, money, and power – just as Lori's prosecutors explained to the jury over the six weeks of her initial trial.

CHAPTER SIX: Trouble on the Horizon

Adam

This is where I believe Lori's beliefs veered past the teachings of the gospel and into deeply troubling, destructive beliefs. Lori didn't always believe in "zombies" – the concept that eventually became the justification she and Chad used for the killings. Nor did she always believe she was a literal god. It began with her association with a certain group of people who wrote and spoke about near death experiences (NDEs), the ability to predict the future, and their ability to speak directly to God for other people.

It's unfortunate that she started following this path so intensely given everything she had going for her at the time. Lori finally had what she'd said she always wanted: a big, happy, eternal family, and marriage to a man who was a faithful member of the Church, an excellent provider, a loving husband, and a devoted father.

I believe Lori was happy for years. Close to a decade, even. But then she became dissatisfied.

So, what changed?

Well, first it's important to know that it didn't happen all at once, and none of her family members knew what was going on at first. From my perspective, Lori gradually transitioned from being a devout, faithful, ordinary 'Mormon' to someone who considered herself something more than ordinary. And as Lori's views of herself changed, so did her views of Charles.

Charles was a good church member. But as Lori became – in her mind – a more spiritual being, a husband who was *just* a good church member wasn't enough.

What caused Lori to believe that she had surpassed her husband – the man she had shared the gospel with – in spirituality?

My answer to that question is: her association with the Prepper movement.

Those readers who are already familiar with Lori's case will probably know that she was closely associated with several groups that are well-known for their 'prepper' behavior.

'Prepper' refers to people from all sorts of communities and religions who are specifically focused on preparing for the Second Coming of Jesus Christ.

Let me be clear here: I'm not condemning the prepper movement. There are plenty of preppers who are good, God-fearing people. But just like everything else in the world, some people take things to extremes. Lori took 'prepping' to extremes.

Here's a little background on where the prepper movement came from, at least for members of the movement who are LDS.

One of the main tenets of the Church of Jesus Christ of Latter-day Saints is that the Second Coming is not far in the future, thus the inclusion of "Latter-day" in the church's name. Our founding prophet, Joseph Smith, declared that we are living in the last days before Christ's return to Earth to punish the wicked, and redeem his people. Many Christians throughout the world hold similar beliefs. Joseph Smith also taught that while we may not know the exact year, hour, or day when Christ will come again, we can still prepare for his imminent arrival.

The Prophet Ezra Taft Benson (August 4, 1899 – May 30, 1994) advised every member family to keep a two-year supply of food storage and have a 72-emergency kit on hand.

Benson's statements are now interpreted by current church administration as simple advice to stay prepared. The reserves he recommended having on hand could be used during anything from a prolonged power outage to a time of financial strain, such as from job loss, illness, or even dire straits brought on by medical expenses.

Some take it further, though. Certain members of our church hear these words as a call to action to prepare for one specific event: the Second Coming of Christ.

The Bible contains many terrifying descriptions of the destruction and devastation that will occur at the time of the Second Coming. These prophecies by ancient prophets have inspired many preppers to be thoroughly dedicated to preparing for apocalypse-level scenarios. They stockpile not only food, but weapons, tech, and even build elaborate bunkers they can use to endure the apocalyptic weather, or whatever metaphorical storm they're anticipating.

Lori had her introduction to the prepper movement right after she read our cousin Braxton Southwick's book, *A Letter to My Friends,* which he self-published in 2012. Braxton wrote the book to explain his perspective on what the end of the world would look like. In it, he talked about how to prepare to live in the last days and what things you would need to survive. He was pretty well known in the prepper community and had even been a guest on a reality TV show about preppers.

After reading Braxton's book, Lori called practically everyone in our family, urging us to take our preparation for the last days seriously. She even sent all of us survival backpacks. I was excited to get mine! It had so many useful things in it, and I hadn't been the best at maintaining emergency food or water storage, even though I can see the wisdom in being prepared for short-term emergencies.

But that's about where the similarity between Lori and Braxton ended, as far as prepping went. Lori didn't care so much about the weapons and ammo and MREs, or about the *physical* preparation for the Second Coming; she was focused on the *spiritual* preparation.

As Lori became more deeply involved with the people who were selling the idea that they had extra authority and insider knowledge because of their NDEs, Lori began to want more than to just survive the Second Coming. She wanted to be instrumental in bringing the Second Coming to pass.

Eventually, her thinking became so twisted, that she professed to believe that she was a god who had been appointed to gather and lead the 144,000 survivors of the Second Coming through the trials and tribulations that would burn the wicked to stubble.

**

My sister's convictions had always been strong. But as she aged, not only did they become stronger, they became greedier, as well. Lori's beliefs had already strayed beyond the tenets of the gospel by the time she met Chad.

In my mind, Lori's beliefs took an abrupt departure from sanity the same time she learned about Julie Rowe. Rowe is a former Latter-day Saint author (she was excommunicated in April of 2019), podcast host, and self-proclaimed clairvoyant. Julie is one of those mentioned earlier who profess to have had prophetic abilities bestowed upon her during her NDE in 2004.

Lori saw Julie's success and wanted some for herself. She was just as spiritual, just as righteous, just as devout. She should be just as special, too. Lori wanted the respect and appreciation she saw others heaping on Julie.

It wasn't long before Lori decided that she'd experienced her own NDE while giving birth to Tylee. It's strange, considering she had such a close bond with her siblings and her parents, that she never told any of us about this when it actually happened, don't you think? We first heard about it during the bizarre, disgusting statement she gave prior to being sentenced for the deaths of Tylee, J.J., and Tammy Daybell. But she'd told plenty of people in her close-knit End of Times group that she, like Rowe, was able to predict the future and see visions.

Guess who Rowe's publisher was? That's right. None other than Chad Daybell.

Daybell was also a (formerly) Latter-day Saint author who claims to have had not just one, but several NDEs, and used that fact to strengthen his own credibility within the prepper community.

You better believe that Lori knew all about Chad and had read all his books well before they met.

CHAPTER SEVEN: The Perfect Storm

Adam

The definition of a perfect storm is:

"A particularly bad or critical state of affairs, arising from a number of negative and unpredictable factors."

Lori meeting Chad was the clearest example of a perfect storm there could be.

It's extremely difficult for me to even try to put into words the rage and loss and hopelessness I experience surrounding the death of my brother-in-law, Charles Vallow and Lori's subsequent marriage to Chad Daybell, of all people.

Chad is the only one of Lori's husbands who I've never met. I'm glad I've never met him. But they were married before I ever even heard of him.

Meeting Chad didn't set her on her path to destruction, he just accelerated her toward the finish.

Even writing that makes me shake my head in absolute bewilderment. *Chad Daybell and my sister.*

I mentioned before that I've never met Chad. I never want to meet Chad. I've never read his books or listened to him speak at conferences or on podcasts – and Braxton has assured me that I'm not missing out on much. I've seen and heard just enough to be astonished that he has a pulse, let alone that he can be some kind of criminal mastermind who orchestrated a plan to take out members of the Cox family one at a time.

To me, Chad is more amphibian than human, but since he does technically qualify as human, I see him as someone who thought very highly of himself despite having very little to recommend him. Maybe he has a great imagination. I hope it serves him well in prison. Maybe he really did have an NDE, or maybe even several. From what I've heard, and not just from Braxton, he's not a great writer. He's not a great businessperson. He certainly wasn't a great husband to his first – now deceased – wife, Tammy. As for how he was as a father, I won't speculate out of respect for his children, who have lost their mother. The one thing I do think Chad had going for him was the ability to manipulate others.

That doesn't mean that I think he manipulated my sister into doing things she didn't want to do. My sister didn't and doesn't take orders from men.

No. Rather, I think Chad had created, over the course of decades, this fantasy about a man who was special…a man who was brilliant, gifted, remarkable, talented, but also unappreciated, often overlooked. Misunderstood. It was like a role-playing fantasy game, or a dystopian fanfic in which he'd cast himself as the hero on a quest fighting against the whole world. And the day my sister, Lori, showed up at his booth at the Preparing a People conference and announced that she was a fan and was going to stay with him and help him sell his books with her bright blue eyes, her big, gorgeous smile, and her captivating charm, was the day Chad believed he'd finally received the reward he'd been waiting for.

"Well done, thy good and faithful servant," I imagine Chad hearing in his head as if it was the voice of God when Lori showered her effervescent attention on him, *"Receive thy reward."*

Shockingly – to me at any rate – all Chad had to do was feed Lori a bit of the nonsense fantasy he'd been telling himself as a bedtime story over the years and cast her as the female lead.

It worked, because Lori had created a similar story in her mind: she was a goddess with a divine mission. She had moved past caring about saving emotionally damaged and unavailable men to believing she had an entire people to gather and save. And not just any people. She believed she was chosen to lead the biblical 144,000 in their mission to save as many sinners as possible during the Last Days before the Second Coming of Christ, and who will reign with Christ in heaven.

Lori fed into Chad's fantasy, and he lit hers on fire.

Lori's state of mind was now becoming clearly delusional, but Chad made her think it was real. With the things Chad told her about her past lives and her seniority of being an elite spirit in previous lives, Lori was sold. In return, she encouraged him in employing his professed spiritual gifts of being able to rank people's spirituality on a light/dark scale and asked him to seek divine guidance in creating a list they could use in their fight against Satan. She also supported his claim that he could ascertain the past-life identities of members of the Church. Lori encouraged Chad to continue this work, which he then presented to members in attempts to recruit them to their cause. At some point, Chad decided to found his own incarnation of the Church of the Firstborn, which historically formed as an offshoot of the Church of Jesus Christ of Latter-day Saints after the death of the prophet and founder Joseph Smith. The sect preached the divinity of Smith as its prophet, and also professed belief in reincarnation.

Talk about the megalomania of these two! Like I said before, Lori didn't change overnight. She didn't go to bed one night as a loving wife, devoted mother, caring sister, faithful church member and wake up the next day as a monster who not only considered murder, but actually conspired and carried out murder. But for me and other members of our family, that's almost what it seemed like.

It wasn't until Lori started sharing about her visions of Christ and Satan that I thought maybe she'd started going off in the weeds spirituality-wise. My concern grew to alarm when she told me in the kitchen that day that she was transforming into an immortal being.

That's when Charles began reaching out to our family members and to law enforcement out of concern for Lori, reporting that she'd told him she no longer cared for him or J.J., and that she was the reincarnated wife of Joseph Smith. He sent emails saying that Lori told him that she knew the real Charles had been possessed by an evil spirit named Ned Schneider, and that she could and would kill Ned. Charles repeated some of Lori's delusional beliefs that she'd shared with me herself in the kitchen that day, such as that she was immortal.

None of that vibes with the Lori I bonded with as a child growing up in our parents' house. Lori hadn't been manipulative. She hadn't been a liar. She had been loyal and loving and determined and her family was her priority.

So, when all of this started, to us, it did seem like it happened over night. I was caught off guard, Charles was caught off guard. The rest of my family was so caught off guard that they simply refused to believe what we were telling them.

Of course, they also had Lori, whispering in their other ear, telling lies. She garnered seemingly unending sympathy when she informed us all that her husband, Charles Vallow, was having an affair.

In reality, of course, *she* was having an affair. With Chad. She further sowed seeds of division in our family by spinning some story about me, my son Zac, and my nephew-in-law, Brandon Boudreaux. She claimed we were trying to kill her and net ourselves a two-million-dollar payout from a life insurance policy. Or that we were working with Kay and Larry Woodcock to kidnap J.J. and give him back to his grandparents.

Concurrently, she was actively planning the death of her husband so that she could net *herself* the one-million-dollar payout of *his* policy. The web of lies that Lori spun was as endless as it was deranged.

And worst of all, it worked on so many people in my family. At least it worked at first, when it mattered the most. Even as I saw it all playing out in real time and actively tried to warn the rest of my family, my bedrock of support, I was met with disbelief and accusations. Suddenly *I* was the liar.

For example, I thought her devout religiosity had veered so far from normal that it warranted some sort of response – an intervention, or a specialist maybe. But when I shared my concerns with my parents, they had a far different take.

"Good heavens," my mom said. "She's going to the temple five hours a day and reading her Bible the rest of it. She's not doing any harm."

It was infuriating. I constantly asked myself how everyone else could be so naive as I watched Lori and Alex intertwine themselves with Chad right in front of our eyes. All the clues were right in front of our faces, but somehow, hardly anyone saw it but me.

Clearly, they didn't want to see. I get that. Who wants to admit that their daughter, their sister, their mom, is capable of such diabolical things?

Charles was among the first to be labeled a 'zombie.' He was also the first to die.

CHAPTER EIGHT: His Sister's Keeper

Adam

Lori and Chad seemed to be the driving force behind these tragedies, but they weren't the only two involved. My brother, Alex, played a vital role in what happened. Of the two, he showed more signs of trouble earlier on than Lori did. I've loved and bonded with my brother for most of my life, but that care has always been overshadowed by something else: worry.

I'll start by tracing that worry back as far as I can, to when it reared its head as my brother, Alex, returned home from serving a full-time mission for The Church of Jesus Christ of Latter-Day Saints. I was worried about him constantly. You see, he'd had a rougher teenage life than others. He was in a car accident when he was 16, and as a result, he had developed a hematoma on his brain. I don't think that was the only damage done. Either way, while the rest of the world moved on, he didn't. To me, he always seemed stuck at 16 on an emotional level at least.

In our early twenties, Alex and I moved to Salt Lake City. We bonded like two brothers should. After a year, I landed a radio job in Austin, Texas, and while Alex went off to California at first, he eventually decided to move to Austin as well. I was happy enough to have him close by, but it did shine a light on that worry that has always lingered since. Alex just didn't seem able to find his drive. A calling in life in which he could apply himself and exhibit ambition of his own. He tried his hand at comedy for a while, and I genuinely thought he was skilled at it. I would have been so proud to see him go off to Vegas and show the world his talent. But it never amounted to more than the occasional stand-up gig at a bar.

So, I kept on worrying. I worried that he would never have a wife and kids. I worried he wouldn't make friends. I worried that he was doomed to be a loner for most of his life. I loved him of course, and he seemed content with his lot in life, but the worry persisted all the same.

Why didn't Alex have many friends? I asked myself that a lot, and as much as I hate to say it, I think it comes down to how much effort it takes to maintain a friendship. I had a lot of friends growing up, and when they came over, Alex was more than happy to talk and hang out with them, so it wasn't that he was asocial. At the same time, them being my friends first meant Alex didn't have to call them, get permission to have them over, arrange a ride, or anything like that. On the one hand, I think he was okay being mostly on his own. He had a couple inconsistent friends here and there, and he loved watching cartoons and TV in general – that's how he got so good at impressions. On the other hand, I can't help but wonder what he was missing out on, how he could have turned out if he'd built more of a support network for himself.

And, while he wasn't lazy, he definitely had trouble keeping a job down. I remember sitting down with him at one o'clock one night, trying to figure out what was going on with his employment history. At one point, I asked him point blank, "Alex, how many jobs have you had in your life?" He started counting. It took a while, because the final amount was well over four hundred.

Four hundred jobs. That might sound made up to some people, but it made all too much sense to me. Alex had a habit of not sticking with anything. If he got a job, showed up for the first few days, and decided he didn't like it, he would just quit.

Again, he seemed content with his situation, but as a brother, it was so hard for me to see so much missed potential just sitting there, unused. I remember thinking when we were kids that he was destined for Las Vegas, or Hollywood, or somewhere he could put his impressions and his knack for comedy to work for him. But it never happened. Did he feel just as unfulfilled as I did for him? Was there a hole in his life that he needed to fill with some greater purpose? It's hard to say, but it would certainly explain some things.

There were two main factors that I think pushed Alex into following Lori down the hellhole they both fell into. First, they were both extremely dedicated to the church. The problem was that Alex had a lot more trouble with following the church's instructions. At the time, Alex was on the path to getting re-baptized after having been excommunicated from our church. It was a hard path for him, but it was also one he'd walked before. Alex had a bad habit of flying down to Columbia to find a woman to marry. He would fly down, party with some girls, then come back feeling so guilty about it that he'd have to confess to his bishop. This got him excommunicated two separate times. Alex loved the church – I genuinely think he wanted to be a good member with all his heart – but he struggled so much with keeping the commandments.

Second, even before the religious angle amplified everything, Alex had always been fiercely protective of Lori, to the point that she could easily manipulate him into doing what she wanted. Chad would play into this by telling him that he was some sort of guardian angel sent to protect Lori, but even before that, Alex was all too eager to do Lori's dirty work.

I've already mentioned that Alex was protective of Lori and gave the example of the time he tased her third husband, Joe Ryan. Here, I'll offer a little more information to illustrate the frightening level of power and influence Lori had over Alex, as the foundation of his reason for identifying as her 'destroying angel'.

Remember that during their custody battle, Lori accused Joe of molesting Colby, her son from a previous marriage, as well as Tylee, the daughter they had together. Obviously, the entire family was heartbroken and outraged to hear those allegations. Lori was furious, like any mom would be, but more than that, she wanted to make Joe pay.

"Which one of you men are going to do something about it?" she asked all of us when she told us what Joe did. She didn't get the responses she was hoping for from most of us. My dad didn't say much, and I was of the opinion that it was up to the police to handle it.

Alex, though, stepped up. "I'll help you," he said. Nobody knew what he meant by that, at least not right away. It would be months before we found out.

Apparently, Alex and Lori spent those months planning. I still don't know all the details, or if everything went the way they wanted it to, but I do know how it played out. One day, when Joe was scheduled to appear at a courthouse for a custody hearing, Alex was there waiting in the parking lot.

"Did you molest Tylee and Colby?" Alex asked him, point blank.

"I would *never* molest those kids. Or any others for that matter," Joe protested.

Alex didn't buy it. He said he could tell Joe was lying just by the look on his face.

So, Alex tased Joe.

I have no idea where he even bought a taser. Either way, Joe called out for help, some people ran over to respond, and Alex was arrested. He served nine months in jail for the assault.

Did Alex regret his actions? Maybe, but not in the way I'd hope. I think he regretted getting arrested, and maybe he regretted whatever plan he cooked up with Lori not playing out perfectly. But the actual assault? He would tell jokes about it afterward in some of his stand-up comedy routines, laughing about how he expected a medal but ended up with jail time instead.

I was left with nothing, save the cold, hard truth that my brother was willing to perform some kind of vigilante justice out of a misguided sense of loyalty to Lori, even though the allegations against Joe were never proven, and were in fact, dismissed. So no, I don't think he regretted what he did.

This is my theory on why Alex chose to follow Lori and Chad. Alex wanted to be a good person. He aspired to be as faithful and devout a member of the church as he thought his little sister was. But he struggled with sin. Sexual sin, specifically. Fornication. Maybe it was impulse control, I don't know, but every time Alex committed what he considered to be a sin, he beat himself up about it and would go to his church leader to confess.

Alex was excommunicated and rebaptized into the Church twice. That's not something that happens very often. Either because people don't self-report, or because they become bitter and defensive once they've been disciplined. But Alex was different. His eternal salvation was very important to him, and he had a strong testimony that the only way he could achieve eternal salvation was as a member in good standing of the Church of Jesus Christ of Latter-day Saint.

Still, after going through the process of excommunication and baptism twice (he was actually baptized three times in total, the first time being at age eight) he continued to struggle with sexual impulses. Alex liked women. He wanted to have a committed relationship, but he didn't seem to have much luck with women reciprocating.

Then, they told him that they'd received revelation that Alex had a more important role to fill other than just following commandments. His mission, they said, was to act as Lori's personal guardian angel. To be her destroying angel, if push came to shove. That he might even be called upon to do things that were normally outside of the laws of men and God. But, as Lori liked to point out, God would rather that one person perish than an entire nation dwindle in disbelief, a concept from both the *Bible* and the *Book of Mormon* that Lori twisted for her own evil purposes.

With this reassurance, Alex felt what I can only imagine to be immense relief. He felt like he had a purpose. He was needed, important. He belonged. It gave him an easy way to live without facing the pressures that usually pushed him off the path he was trying to walk.

CHAPTER NINE: The Worst of All Outcomes

Adam

It's crazy to think that Lori and I, who had been so close growing up, had grown so far apart. By July of 2019, it had been well over a year since she told me she was turning into an immortal being and couldn't be killed, and subsequently began spreading lies about me.

I'd been speaking with Charles, as I mentioned earlier. This is where we pick up on that story, the story of my brother Alex murdering my brother-in-law, Charles.

Charles had already spoken with law-enforcement authorities about some of Lori's more troubling threats and behaviors. He'd requested a psychological screening, which Lori had complied with. But, despite the alarming allegations Charles was making, most everyone who interacted with Lori insisted nothing was wrong with her. She smiled and flirted and charmed, and passed any tests or screenings they threw at her.

After 13 years of marriage, Charles and Lori were separated at this point, but not divorced. Charles and I decided to contact their Stake President. A Stake President is a high-ranking ecclesiastical leader within the Church of Jesus Christ of Latter-day Saints.

Charles and I reasoned that if we could get Lori to agree to speak with her Stake President while one or both of us were present, we could get her help. Lori maintained that she was an active member of the Church of Jesus Christ of Latter-day Saints, yet the things she was saying were in no way connected with the Church's teachings. If she was fabricating the things she was saying for some personal gain, she'd have to make a choice between lying in front of us, or lying to him. If, on the other hand, she truly believed the things she'd said to me and to Charles, the Stake President could corroborate our story and we could get input from the rest of our family about next steps.

Charles bought me a plane ticket, and I flew to Arizona so we could nail down the details of our plan. He kept saying to me, "This is my last-ditch effort, my last thing to try and save Lori and our marriage." If we couldn't get her in front of the Stake President, Charles didn't think he had a chance of reconciling with her and saving their family.

Charles warned me that if Lori found out I was coming to Arizona, she might run. At this time, my parents, Lori, Alex, and even my son, Zac, were all living in Arizona near one another. I told my parents and Alex that I was coming to visit Zac. I even called Alex to mention that it had been a while since we had hung out, and

I'd love to stay at his place while I was in town so we could catch up.

Alex said it was a great idea and that he'd go out and buy a mattress so I could stay in one of his guest rooms. He seemed excited. At the time, I had no way of knowing how deeply Lori had her claws sunk into my brother.

Charles booked a flight for me so that I would arrive in Arizona on Wednesday, July 10, 2019. The "plan" at this point was that I was going to stay with Alex. Charles had to pick up J.J. and take him to school the next day, Thursday. He also told me he was going to spend some time with J.J. but I didn't know any other details besides that. He said he'd text me once he knew more.

As soon as I landed, I texted Alex, but didn't receive a response. My parents came and picked me up from the airport, and I mentioned to them that I was supposed to stay with Alex. I kept calling and texting for the next several hours, but still got no response. My parents said they hadn't heard from him, either, heightening my concern. I ended up staying the night at their place, though I had trouble sleeping; the anxiety of not knowing what was going on with my own brother was intense, to say the least.

The next morning, I got a text from Charles saying he was at Lori's to pick up J.J. and that Alex's truck was parked in front of her house.

I was shocked. If Alex was around, why hadn't he returned my calls or answered my texts? Why was he at Lori's house when he was supposed to be with me?

I just didn't feel right about any of it. The only thing I could think of was that Alex was there as some kind of protection for Lori. *But protection from what?* I wondered. *From Charles? Or was he there to intimidate him?*

Charles was soft spoken and well-mannered. He wasn't in the least bit aggressive. He didn't have any need to be; his presence was imposing enough. I couldn't imagine Charles ever being intimidated by Alex.

It just didn't add up.

I texted Charles, "They're planning something."

"Absolutely," Charles responded.

A knot formed in my stomach as I waited for word of their interaction – if there'd even been one. When I never heard back from Charles, I assumed it hadn't been a big deal and that he was spending time with J.J. like he had mentioned.

Never could I have imagined that "Absolutely" would be the last word I would ever receive from Charles.

I wouldn't find out until several days afterward that Alex had shot Charles at close range in what Alex claimed was self-defense. Both my parents and my sister knew, but neither bothered to tell me. I didn't find out until a friend of mine looked his name up for me. When he told me he'd found a news article stating that Charles had been shot by his brother-in-law, I thought at first it was a bad joke. When I saw the article myself, I broke down.

There's no way Alex shot Charles in self-defense, I told myself.

I was still in shock over losing my close friend, maybe even denial, but I knew with some kind of morbid certainty that Alex and Lori were lying. Their stories didn't add up. Nothing added up. And my friend was dead.

Rex

In March 2019, when we received the emails that Charles sent to family members seeking help with Lori's delusions, I was concerned right away. I recognized some of the same elements in those writings from Chad that I'd seen echoed among the fringe groups of the Mormon Church. I don't know if the words of those particular preachers ever led to murder, but their teachings digressed to a ridiculous degree in an attempt to gain a following and to be seen as being important. They wanted followers – they wanted to be important. That last part sounds especially familiar now.

Since I had no access to Lori when Charles sent those emails, I talked with her mother, Janis. Janis said the division was ugly, and that she believed all of Lori's accusations about Charles. She didn't, however, have access to Lori either, since Lori had cut-off communications with her.

The night before Charles was shot in July 2019, was memorable. I happened to be in town (Gilbert, AZ) and was staying with one of my daughters. Adam and Zac stopped by for a very welcome visit. Of course, the conversation quickly turned to why

Adam was in town from Kansas. The added information about Adam heard Lori espousing, and as observed by Zac from his time living with Lori, was alarming. They shared the threats Lori had made to Charles. That helped me realize why the bits of Lori's stories I had heard were not adding up.

Adam already shared that he and Charles had discussed making a plan to try to record Lori and get her to talk with her Stake President, whom Adam knew. Charles, at that point, was grasping for anything to break Lori out of the apparent trance she was in. He thought if the Stake President would revoke her Temple Recommend, which he thought was her most important possession, it might wake her up to the absurdity of the situation – and of her beliefs. Adam and Charles were going to try to arrange that 'intervention' of sorts the next day after Charles spent some time with J.J.

The next morning, the doubtful story was that Charles went to confront Lori, and Alex intervened. Shortly after Charles arrived at the house, Lori left with Tylee and J.J., leaving Alex and Charles alone together. According to Alex, Charles attacked him with a baseball bat, leaving Alex with no choice but to defend himself. He shot Charles twice in the chest. A clear-cut case of self-defense.

We later learned that Alex waited around 40 minutes before calling 911. Alex claimed it had only been a few minutes. It's also believed he never rendered aid to Charles in spite of the 911 operator walking him through how to administer CPR.

The next I heard about the events there in Arizona was three days later, when my brother called to ask what I knew about the death of Charles Vallow. My mind raced as I reached out to other family members, including Janis, to get more information. Those I talked to had also heard about Lori's recent actions and threats to Charles. Of the at least five family members with whom I discussed it, Janis was the only one who believed that Charles was shot in self-defense. By the time I decided that I had a chance to get some insights from Alex, though, I couldn't reach him. He had already left on a previously planned trip to Colombia. I never got to talk with Alex again.

The fact that the police would allow him to leave town, especially to travel to South America, was mind boggling. Those few who believed the self-defense story held it up as obvious evidence that the shooting was justified. The division in the family had now begun. Since there was very little information available, many of us discussed the situation only with those we agreed with. We were all hoping for details and facts, but that has been an agonizing wait, much of which continues through to today.

Things only got worse from there.

Adam

On August 31, 2019, Lori and her kids packed their things and moved to an apartment complex in Rexburg, Idaho. You might remember that as the same city that Chad Daybell resided in. She wasn't the only one to move; Alex decided to join, and he even lived in the same apartment complex as Lori.

It's around this time that Kay and Larry Woodcock start to lose contact with J.J. and Lori. Lori eventually stopped responding to Kay and Larry altogether, severing their connection to J.J. The last time anyone saw Tylee and J.J. alive together was September 8, from a photo retrieved from Lori's iCloud account. The photo was taken at Yellowstone National Park and shows Tylee and J.J. with their uncle, Alex. In the photo, you can see Tylee and J.J. smiling and holding on to one another.

Sometime in November, Kay logged into Charles' email account using one of the passwords he always used. She saw different Amazon orders that had been delivered to Idaho – including a malachite wedding ring. Using this information, she contacted Rexburg Police and asked them to conduct a welfare check on the kids.

When the police arrived, Lori claimed Tylee and J.J. were with a friend in Arizona.

More people continued to ask Lori where her children were, either on the phone or in person. She always insisted that Tylee and J.J. were safe and happy. Anytime she was pressed to give their location, whatever she said always turned out to be a lie.

The moment Rexburg Police announced that Tylee and J.J. were missing, I knew they were dead. With what had happened to Charles and the way Lori had been manipulating everyone, I knew in my heart that the children weren't just missing. They were gone. In my mind, there was no reason why Lori wouldn't produce the kids, other than the fact that they were already gone.

I reached out to everyone in my family, but my parents and siblings had cut me off. They believed that Lori was just hiding the kids in Hawaii. I felt so lonely and frustrated because my own family had effectively exiled me and wouldn't listen to anything I had to say.

Based on the evidence we have now, it's likely that Tylee and J.J. were killed within the first few weeks of moving to Idaho. Cell phone data showed Alex in Chad's backyard twice that month – in the same locations investigators would eventually find J.J. and Tylee's bodies. It's easy to believe that Alex was there to bury the remains, but we never got the chance to ask him. Alex died before the announcement about the missing children was made.

In 2020, Lori and Chad started the year as newlyweds who could go and do what they wanted, when they wanted. They no longer had their spouses or their children to worry about. They were married in Hawaii, on the same beach where Lori used to take her children years before. Lori was finally arrested on February 20th after failing to produce her children as ordered by the court. Chad was arrested in June on the same day the remains were discovered on his property.

For the short period between their marriage and the first arrest, the world watched as reporters followed the pair around sunny paradise, asking over and over where the kids had gone. Chad and Lori didn't seem to care.

Rex

By the time Tylee and J.J. were publicly declared missing in late December 2019, everything was already spiraling out of control. Chad's wife, Tammy, died; Lori and Chad got married; Tammy's body was *exhumed*; and a day later, Alex died.

It was ridiculous to us that some people failed to recognize the obvious pattern. Some family members were in denial, while a few just held out hope that Tylee and J.J. might eventually turn up. The rest of us would have loved to have been proven wrong, but we could see no way that Lori hadn't killed her children.

J.J.'s special needs would have made it impossible to keep him hidden anywhere. Even if they had, there was no way that Tylee would have disappeared from her friends, family, and social media for any period of time. If you knew Tylee, you knew that several someones would have heard from her had she been alive.

Even with such a clear grasp on the tragically obvious reality, none of us were prepared for the children's bodies being found on Chad's property – or the manner in which their bodies were desecrated and disposed of. Those haunting details will remain with us – with everyone around the world who bore witness – for the rest of our days.

CHAPTER TEN: A Family Destroyed

Adam

There are so many tragedies in this story. I find it hard to just focus on one thing when so many other thoughts are coming to mind.

I know every family has struggles, devastation, hurt feelings, trust issues, and more. I know families that have had members steal money from each other. I know families that have kids with drug problems. I know families that have to deal with sexual abuse. I know families who have to deal with constant lying. I know families that have spouses and kids with cancer and other deadly diseases. I know families that have severely handicapped children or spouses.

As you read this, you probably either know a family that has to deal with something similar or live in one yourself. You are who this book is written for.

I hope and pray that when you start dealing with surprises in your family, you can keep an open mind and heart. It is so easy to just accept or believe a loved one without looking at the whole picture. Don't ever cut anyone off without investigating everything, even if it seems ridiculous at the time. Don't just take family members' word if it feels off. Don't ever get caught thinking I'm not even going to entertain that possibility. Being cut off is one of the most isolating things you can experience, especially when it's for something you know is right but everyone else is insisting is wrong. The bottom line is check for yourself when claims are made about a family member. Even if those claims end up being true, isn't it better to do your own due diligence to determine that for yourself rather than just hope the other voices in your family are correct? If you don't, and the other voices *are* wrong, you'll be casting out someone whose only crime was to be brave enough to speak out about something.

I should know; it's exactly what happened to me.

As I said before, our family was far from perfect. But from what some have said during and after the deaths of Tylee and J.J., you'd think we were a pack of monsters. As I have read, heard, and seen, countless so-called family members have written books, started podcasts about this case, and commented about our family. That includes cousins who were hardly ever around and knew nothing of our family, to sisters-in-law that spent barely any time around us at all. At best, they've gotten some very key details very wrong. At worst, they've tried to cash in on this case all while accusing others of the same thing.

So that's one thing you should learn from this: don't believe everything you read or hear on the internet. I've been in the media – through radio – for 30 years, and there is just so much deception. The media is chewed gum stuck on the bottom of the truth shoe. The best way to get the truth of a story is to take the emotion out of it. Analyze who is presenting it and what their motive is. Ask questions. Listen to the answers you get, and then ask yourself: what makes the most sense to you? Common sense should play a role in your decision making.

This was a time of lies and confusion for our family, no doubt about that. It was only exacerbated by so many of our family members getting duped by the lies and adding to the confusion by failing to conduct their own research and try to understand things for themselves. It got me thinking: how could Lori so easily get away with her lies and her pattern of cutting people off? Why would family members believe her, especially as her behavior got more erratic and spread to include saying she met Jesus face-to-face? I think it all comes down to family members really wanting to believe Lori; they had for most of their lives, so why stop now?

Never in my wildest dreams or nightmares did I think that my family would cut me off. Even if I had, nothing could have helped me predict how low it would bring me. I've never felt as confused or alone as I did when it happened. My family had always been a constant throughout my life, an ever-dependable source of support, love, and security. I think I had a knot in my stomach for months after they cut me off. Maybe even a year.

Had I taken my family, my support structure, for granted? I had always felt like a bit of a golden child, I suppose, like I was the favorite. Maybe that's part of what left me feeling so blindsided.

***

I had a huge decision to make: which interviews would I give? I had every news outlet trying to interview me, and yet, at first, I didn't feel like I wanted to say anything. I was still in shock, and the fate of the kids was still unknown. I had my opinions and theories, of course, but I wasn't ready to tell the world yet.

Now, looking back on things, I find myself thinking more and more about that decision not to speak. It certainly came with its own consequences; because I didn't give any interviews or statements about what I thought, I had random people email me and message me on Facebook and Instagram. They were not messages of support. In fact, many went so far as to accuse me of being a part of it.

Is the takeaway, then, that people should cave to media requests to stop themselves from being harassed? That seems like a bleak conclusion to me. In an ideal world, shouldn't people have the complete right to decide if and when they tell their story?

Of course, we don't live in an ideal world, and coming forward to tell your story – especially *this* kind of story – can be daunting to say the least. Obviously, I eventually came around on the idea; otherwise, I wouldn't be here, sharing all of this with all of you. But it took a while to overcome my reluctance.

A big part of my initial hesitation had to do with the sheer overwhelming sensation that comes with being caught in a media firestorm. I understand why the media was so interested in this story – I've been a radio host for 30 years and have interviewed plenty of athletes and celebrities myself. I also have tried to get interviews from normal people in not-so-normal real-life stories. So, it made perfect sense as to why so many news outlets, shows, podcasts, and documentary producers reached out to me; I would have done the same thing if the roles were reversed. Nevertheless, I was bombarded with requests to respond, give interviews, or even chat off the record. I know everyone has a job to do, and for the most part, they just want to learn more about the story they're reporting on, but this was becoming an avalanche – and I was getting buried quickly. Fox, NBC, ABC, CBS, Dr. Oz, Dr. Phil, Dateline, 20/20, and even Court TV all reached out. And still, I chose not to speak. I wish other members of my family had made the same decision – felt the same reluctance that I did.

When Lori and Chad were in Hawaii, and the kids were still missing, my mom and sister, Summer, got talked into going on TV and doing an interview. They made a *huge* mistake. First, they didn't know enough to go on record and give an interview about Lori. It takes training and experience to be in that kind of situation, and they had neither. Moreover, they had every reason to know that Lori was out of her mind because I had been warning them about it since this all started. By this point, I knew with chilling confidence that Alex murdered Charles – and not in self-defense like so many members of my family still seemed to believe. I knew what they were doing was evil. But my parents didn't want to listen. They still thought Alex was an angel for 'protecting' Tylee from Charles. They were not going to start listening to me now.

So, my mom and Summer went on ABC 20/20 and did an interview about Lori.

When I saw this on TV, I was screaming. When I heard the answers they were giving, it got worse. On air, they said that Lori would never hurt Tylee and J.J. No one knew they were dead yet, and I only had my suspicions, but I definitely didn't believe any of the excuses that Lori or Alex gave. If your children are missing, and the authorities say, 'tell us where your kids are so we can know that they are safe or you're going to jail,' you *should* tell them. If you don't, and you further don't even seem to care about their wellbeing, that, to me, implies you killed or at least hurt them and can't tell the police where they are. Period. I'd done my best to try and warn my mom and sister about how wrong they were, and still they went on T.V. to repeat Lori's lies. I was furious.

I think that fury is part of what started to push me toward speaking. At this point, there was no proof of what I was believing – I just had my gut feeling and my common sense – so I didn't want to fall into the same trap as my mom and sister. On the other hand, I couldn't bear their words representing our whole family.

So, I gave one appearance as part of a documentary that was about the case and mostly about the kids, Tylee and J.J. I was approached by A&E productions and decided that I would participate in this documentary because I wanted my side of the story to be out there. I'd seen too many news stories where the reporters were just speculating or getting the facts wrong, and I wanted to ensure that the record included my experience, not just that of my mom and sister.

I flew down to record several hours in an Airbnb house in south St George, where I was greeted by a film crew who had set up cameras and big microphones around the kitchen and dining area in this house. I sat down in a chair facing the main camera and had a big light shining in my face. I started to answer questions about every topic associated with Lori's case. In total, I was there answering questions for about four hours. Then I left and waited.

The documentary finally came out after several months of waiting. It used about five minutes' worth of my four-hour interview. That is how TV works, but I won't pretend I wasn't frustrated.

Still, I felt I'd gotten to say my piece at least, so as more requests for interviews came in after the documentary, I still denied them all. Those five minutes of interview that made it to air were good enough for me.

As time passed and story after story flooded the news, though, I became less and less satisfied. I had more to say, and I wanted to be the one in charge of how it came out. So, I decided to do a podcast with my son, Zac. Zac lived with Charles and Lori for several months, and I felt it was important for him to share the things he experienced while living there.

During our two-hour podcast with a company out of Canada, we told the truth. I even tried to explain in that podcast about how Alex and Lori wanted Joe dead. Joe was Lori's third husband, whom, we were all told by Lori, sexually abused Lori's children, Tylee and Colby. Following Lori and Joe's divorce, Lori and Alex frequently talked about how they planned "to get" Joe. J. We all thought they were just talking trash. That part of the interview sounded weird after listening to it back. When the podcast finally aired, those who listened to it were offered more information that could help them understand the situation more fully. Making that a reality was intensely gratifying. It's a big part of why Uncle Rex and I went on to start our own podcast series.

It also chipped away further at my reluctance to talk in general. The A&E documentary had been a bit of a bust, but I'd had the opportunity to tell my story on my terms now, and I wanted more. As such, I accepted an opportunity to do a 20/20 special about the case. I flew to Los Angeles California in November of 2021 to film it.

The reason I went with ABC's 20/20 among the plethora of other requests I received is because they convinced me I would be able to tell my story like I had with the podcast episode. ABC's 20/20 ended up calling the episode " Adam and Evil." That was not my favorite title for the show, but they didn't ask me my opinion. I did, however, like how they edited our interview and presented it. There are so many layers to this story. I'm sure people get confused.

Now that the kids have been found and Lori's trial is over, we have a better understanding of what happened. With that knowledge comes *some* closure, but not without yet more terrible pain. The deaths were brutal. There is no escaping or downplaying that, as much as it mattered for the details to come out in full. Even with closure, we all want – need – relief from the pain and heartache the events of the past few years have steeped upon us. Writing this book helps me unload some of my frustrations and emotions. I am on a daily search to find peace and comfort to help me cope with all the loss. My hope is one day to wake up one morning and not have this tragedy be the first thing on my mind.

As part of that journey toward healing, I'm glad I decided to tell my story. That's not to say I regret my initial hesitancy; I don't know what good would have come out of me doing an interview circuit with every media group under the sun back when I was getting bombarded with requests. But part of healing is sharing, and sharing my story with the world has been vitally important to me and Rex. If you have tragedy in your life, it is absolutely your prerogative to decide if and when you'll speak about it. Don't feel pressured to hop on every interview opportunity you get, or at the smaller scale, to share your most haunting moments with anyone who asks. But know that you don't have to go it alone. You don't have to keep it bottled up inside. So, if you get the chance to share your story, and especially if you can own your own story and how it's told, keep your mind open to the possibility of sharing the load with others. Take it from me: there are some awesome people out there who have also been hurt and who won't hesitate to listen, commiserate, and truly *heal* with you.

PART THREE: Picking up the Pieces

CHAPTER TEN: Unique Paths to Healing

Rex

The first time the thought crossed my mind that I would need to heal from this entire experience was while sitting in the courtroom listening to the forensic pathologist go into vivid detail about the death of J.J.

Until that day, my wife and I had intentionally stayed away from the details about how the children actually died, knowing that level of information would be too much for us to handle. We hadn't even discussed it much among ourselves or others in the family. As we were forced to learn more, we took a miniscule amount of comfort in the idea that Tylee and J.J. had been poisoned, gone to sleep, and just never woke up. It was still a tragic idea, but it at least meant the deaths were peaceful. Then, when the bodies were discovered, we hoped they had just had a rushed burial performed by arrogantly stupid criminals in Chad's yard.

To this day, the thought that J.J., Tylee, and even Tammy had to fight for their lives during their last few moments on Earth fills me with profound sadness.

As we all listened to the details in the courtroom that day, I did not have any idea how to process this gruesome new information I was now trying to digest. During those moments, I looked at my daughter Melissa's face, who was sitting next to me, and recognized the state in which I needed to be just to cope with the moment and get through it. Even though we were not supposed to interact during testimony in the courtroom, I whispered, "What are you experiencing right now?" Without changing her expression, or even glancing my way, she responded, "I am so *enraged* right now."

That was it. It was rage that was building up inside of me:

Rage at the murderer who put the bag over J.J.'s head.

Rage at whoever was holding him down as he used his extraordinary upper-body strength to struggle against people who were supposed to love him.

Rage at the discovery that the forensic pathologists couldn't even speculate at the cause of Tylee's death because her body had not just been dismembered, but brutally hacked to pieces and attacked with tools that would inflict pain and mutilation.

Rage at the realization that Tylee had been living in fear during her last who-knows-how-many days of her life, carrying the secrets she carried and not finding a way to escape them.

Rage that Alex was left to roam free after such flimsy, conflicting stories were offered after he shot Charles.

Rage to hear that Tammy had been snuffed out while in her own bed while she was held down to render her helpless.

Rage to realize that there were probably more than the three co-conspirators already known, who weren't rotting either in jail or in the grave where they belonged.

That is a lot of rage for me to experience. Since I can't recall ever previously experiencing rage in my life, I had no idea how I was going to handle it. But it was, somewhat to my surprise, my immediate ally. I clung to it like a hungry dog to a bone just to cope with the avalanche of emotions I was now experiencing for the first time.

Even at that point, as the thought first crossed my mind, I didn't fully appreciate the need for healing that this signaled. I think my first indication that I needed some form of reconciliation with my prior self was when the profound sadness, or grief that was being masked by that rage I felt, prevented me from living my day-to-day life. I'm not referring to *all* the emotions involved; I hope to never reach a point at which I'm not saddened by the loss of the victims or the injustices that surround their loss. I'm referring to losing or straining relationships, or refusing to participate in certain activities because of who might be there or what the activities might bring to my memory. For example, to this day, my wife and I don't want to risk the emotional burden we might feel by simply watching an emotional movie – even an uplifting one. If I'm not healthy enough to watch a movie without risking a crisis, then I obviously have some work to do. Fortunately, the healing had begun before I knew I needed it and before I even recognized it as healing.

I hadn't felt the need to attend Lori's trial, but when three of my daughters decided they needed to experience it, I volunteered to go with them to share expenses, to shuttle them to and from the courthouse, and to process with them. We rented a house for the three days we would be there, giving us a place to sit around and just process our feelings together after each day we were in court.

That kind of processing had proven to be the best way for us to cope since Charles' death kicked off a long year of tragedies. My five children spent a lot of time doing so together, especially the four daughters, and they've since included me and their mom. I processed with my wife and with Adam, along with the children. Within each of us, the desire to talk about what we were experiencing, to get more details, and to share it outside of that circle, would ebb and flow. Since talking about this kind of emotional event had been our practice, it was natural to continue that while we were at the trial.

Our second of the three days in court was the same day that Summer, Lori's sister, testified. My three girls and Summer all live in the Phoenix area and were surprised to find themselves on the same flight to the trial in Boise. We arrived and exited the courthouse with Summer and her husband, Jeff. Together, we all experienced something none of us were prepared for: an intense amount of public scrutiny.

There were many members of the media outside of the courtroom, all intensely interested in any tidbit of information or reactions they could glean from people in the courtroom during the trial. Since no one from Lori's family had attended the trial before us, we were singled out as possessing a fresh perspective that hadn't been examined yet. Summer, Jeff, and my three daughters wanted no part of media interviews, just as most people want no part of the public spotlight for a variety of personal reasons.

I, on the other hand, really don't mind the process. So, knowing that it doesn't really bother me, my daughters and I agreed that I would make myself available to any interested members of the media while the rest of my family escaped in the background.

At this point, I have to acknowledge a story within the story. Nate Eaton, a Dateline NBC contributor and the news director at East Idaho News, has earned a revered place within our family as the face of the media we could trust with any aspect of the story. Of course, Nate became associated with the story early on when he unapologetically tracked down Lori and Chad in Hawaii and would not stop asking them, "Where are your children?" He has passionately and compassionately followed the story ever since.

After the children's murdered bodies were found, Summer organized two memorial services in Gilbert, Arizona for friends and family of Tylee and J.J., and Nate called Summer to ask if he could attend. Summer politely declined, saying she didn't want any press coverage detracting from the purpose of the event. So, Nate asked if he could just come as a participant to honor the memories of Tylee and J.J. and to meet many of the people whose lives they touched during their shortened lives. He said he wouldn't be there as a reporter. He came and was good to his word, abstaining from covering the event and instead respectfully joining us in our mourning. That act of sincerity endeared him to all of us in the family.

That's not to say that my interactions with other reporters were wholly negative. Our entry to the courthouse on the first morning was through a side entrance with a Bailiff escort because of Summer being a witness, so the media members couldn't really access us at that time. Leaving the courthouse that first day was a different story. By then, reporters knew my daughters and I were family members of Lori and, of course, requested reactions from us. As agreed, I stopped and talked to the first reporter while the girls escaped to the car.

Over the course of the three days, I did at least a dozen interviews, and it soon became more than just a cover for the girls to escape the exposure. I found myself *wanting* to do interviews because in them, I found a purpose and maybe even some level of fulfillment.

That purpose became obvious to me the first day we attended the trial. When we entered the courtroom for the first time, our perspectives changed immediately.

First of all, Lori was right there! It was not a large room, and we were seated by our very helpful victim's advocate, Whitney, immediately behind a detective, who himself was immediately behind the prosecution team. That put us three rows back from Lori and her defense team, for a total of about 25-30 feet. Being so close to her after all this time, after learning about everything she'd done, was a surreal experience. Our immediate reaction upon seeing her was, "There's Lolo with whom we have shared so many endearing experiences," but just as quickly turned to, "the Lori we knew and loved is now gone. This person sitting in the courtroom has perpetrated evil beyond comprehension."

The next new perspective had to do with how many people were involved in this effort to find justice for Tylee, J.J., Tammy, and Charles – which served as a much more positive experience. Just in that room, there were more than a dozen people on the court staff and legal teams, including four bailiffs. There were 18 jurors, six of which were alternates but still had to fully participate. The detective in front of me was Ray Hermosillo, who we came to see as the face of the army of law enforcement members who dedicated so much time, energy, emotion, and caring to finding justice for these victims. The media personnel in the room represented an army of people also exerting their professional efforts in pursuit of the goal of justice. Later, when I started reading comments on the many news postings and interviews associated with this case, I added to my list of realizations the millions of people who have connected with this case from all over the world.

Just knowing that this vast amount of people and their personal emotions, energies, and efforts were all combining for this cause overwhelmed me. I don't know how, but I know my heartfelt gratitude went out to all of them all around the world, all at once. I don't really know if that's a thing, but I can't be convinced it is not.

My purpose now, in doing interviews, and later in doing the podcast and in contributing to this book is to thank ALL of those people, all of YOU from all over the World, who has united in the purpose of finding justice for the victims. That includes all of the victims, both living and dead, who have been scarred by this evil.

Ultimately, my healing had begun.

It occurred to me as we frequently discussed healing on our podcast that my healing may never be finished. Frankly, I'm not even sure what it means to be healed from this kind of emotional injury, but maybe that is not the point. The fact that my healing started with that realization in the courtroom and has continued though processing with family members, by doing a podcast on the subject, by writing this book, by doing countless interviews and having countless conversations about the case with friends and strangers, and by complementing all that with professional counseling, doesn't serve anyone but me. I am inexpressibly grateful for all of the love, concern, and healing from which I have benefitted through this process, but the purpose we hope to achieve by sharing this book with you is for you to get whatever will benefit you from it.

Just as we are each an individual in life with our own DNA and fingerprints, our experiences in life are completely unique. Our reactions to those experiences are unique. I believe it follows that our definition of what healing is and our path to receiving that healing is also unique for each of us.

To whatever degree that is accurate, or to whatever degree you believe that, it presents a foundationally important question:

How do I know what I need, then how do I get it?

We've been fortunate enough to cultivate an absolutely wonderful group of listeners to our podcast. These optimists (more on that in an addendum to this book) and our interactions with them have left us convinced of a couple of life's realities:

Most everyone has to deal with personal, family, and/or traumatic tragedies in life.

Most everyone who has taken an ongoing interest in this case is looking to take away something personal, even if it's just an increased understanding of how a tragedy like this could happen.

Everyone's definition of, and experience with, what they need in this context is uniquely personal.

You aren't going to get the definitive answer about what you need from another person, are you? No matter how well they know and/or love you, how could they know better than you? They can make suggestions to you until they hit on what resonates with you, but **the resonating is the important clue.**

You can only know definitively what you need by listening when your internal guidance system confirms it for you.

How do you get what you need?

The answer to this question will be the same as the answer to the last question. With all of the wonderful, well-meaning, tried-and-true advice, formulas, professional insights, and counsel available to you, the only valid confirmation of what will result in what you need will come from your internal guidance system – your conscience, your intuition, whatever you choose to call it.

That statement should not be construed to mean you should ignore all of the resources available to you. What I've described above is simply the most efficient and effective process that nature has provided to answer this question. Start with your own awareness as you pose the question to yourself, then remain immersed in that awareness as you explore the options that life has presented to you. Return to that awareness of your internal guidance every time you realize that your reasoning, or your ego, or your appetites, or your fears have hijacked the decision-making process and caused confusion. And keep returning – every time.

Please note that all of the advice you have not received in this chapter of the book. You have not been advised to:

- Handle your family situations like Adam handled his.
- Read a specific book (even this one).
- Listen to a certain podcast (even ours), or guru.
- Look to religion, science, medicine, psychology, or other disciplines of studying life.
- Get professional or paraprofessional counseling.
- Get answers from others with similar experiences or needs.

You *have* been advised to access your own internal guidance system, follow where it leads you, and return to following that whenever you find yourself straying from the path it prescribed to you.

CHAPTER ELEVEN: Avoiding Pitfalls

Rex

After all the pain and heartache she inflicted, after her ultimate betrayal of the two people who should have been able to trust her the most, Lori was finally found guilty of the murder of Tylee and J.J., and guilty of conspiracy to murder Tammy Daybell. She was sentenced to five life sentences on July 31st, 2023.

I was present for the tidal wave of emotions released at Lori's hearing. Once again, the decision to be present was a difficult one. Ultimately, my wife, Lisa, and I decided at 8:30 p.m. the previous evening to make the eight-hour drive to Idaho to be in attendance. Before we left, I texted the very kind Victim's Advocate, Whitney, who confirmed we could be seated in the courtroom.

The experience was ultimately healing. To be reunited with such a large, loving group of people who were all searching for justice for the victims, and for some way to make sense of the tragedy, was such a unique lifetime event. There was so much love and support shared that I couldn't help but feel restored in some way. As such, I'd like to take some time to thank everyone involved in that healing. I think it's especially important to do so – to focus on the bright parts of that day – given what else came out of that courtroom.

My heart and thanks go out to Kay and Larry Woodcock, J.J.'s grandparents, who acted as gravitational centers of this whole loving exchange. They started the chain of events that made this tragedy public when they first requested that the Rexburg police perform a wellness check for their grandson, J.J., whom they had not been able to contact through Lori. They soon became the face of the nationwide effort to find the missing children – and the worldwide effort to bring justice to their murderers. Larry and Kay are wonderful examples of giving love to, and receiving love from, everyone around them.

A few breaks in the proceedings also gave me the chance to once again express very sincere thanks to the many law enforcement members and their families who attended the sentencing. They represented an army of professionals who had been involved in the case and who had ultimately contributed to finding the children and bringing their murderers to justice.

Many of those in law enforcement present at the sentencing were also present on Chad's property as part of the team digging through the dirt to find evidence of the children. Just as with military service members who have to experience traumatizing realities humans just shouldn't have to encounter in this life, there's just not an adequate way to thank the people who do this for us all.

It was also a chance to thank the many people involved in the legal process required to bring as much justice as possible to those guilty of these horrors. The judge, the judge's staff, and both the prosecution and defense teams are all a very positive part of the system.

Yes, I'm grateful even for the defense team, which includes many people behind the scenes. While I didn't care for much of what they said or did during the proceedings, I appreciate that they afforded Lori every right she is entitled to under our system of justice. After all, how could we have said justice was served against Lori if she hadn't received an adequate, competent defense? My sincere thanks I gave to those with whom I spoke sounded something like: "Thank you for doing what you were obligated to do, even though Lori gave you virtually nothing to work with."

After the sentencing, there was a media frenzy outside of the courthouse. I continued to represent our family and participated in each of the many interviews requested of me. Was I unconsciously motivated by the need for attention, as has been suggested by some who follow this story, especially after my appearance at the trial itself? Maybe. Though in truth, I feel like I get all of the positive attention I need in my life from the people who are most important to me. Maybe there's a subconscious desire for more, but I hope that is not my primary motive in being willing to share my perspective on what has happened.

One of the first overwhelming realizations that overcame me while attending the trial sessions three months prior to this was how far this horrendous story had spread around the world. The comments on the interviews were from dozens of countries from all parts of the globe. And, beautifully, all those comments are from people who are truly on the same side. We all just want justice for the victims of this tragedy. Even if there's some minor disagreement on what that justice should look like, there is no one crying for the release of Chad and Lori. We are all united.

Wow. In this day of rampant division, here is a tragedy that unites all of us. No one involved in this cause cares about the others' political or religious views, where they live, or their sexual orientation. I also witnessed the same army of media, which carries those often-divisive messages, reporting the facts of this event in a truthful, unifying manner.

I understand why so many people don't want to interact with the media. It is especially difficult for people close to the victims and others inside the story to deal with the emotions and scrutiny that comes with media exposure. In recognition of and with respect for that, here is an army of media trying to share any information they can, trying to get that information from people who are hesitant to share it.

Being near the front lines, I witnessed how tough and often thankless this responsibility truly is. Yet the worldwide outpouring of love, and all of the healing that accompanies it, is dependent on those media sources. Upon realizing that, I was filled with an intense desire to respond to any media requests from anyone who thought I could contribute to their story. By doing so, I hoped to contribute to the healing I know *I* need, and which I believe we all need to some degree.

Every opportunity I get to interact with people in the media is an opportunity to thank them for their role in my healing and in our healing.

There are doubtlessly countless people I'm forgetting to thank, but doing so could take up an entire book. And we still have statements made during the court proceedings to discuss. There was quite the range of emotions on display inside that courtroom.

Each victim impact statement provided plenty of opportunities for healing for both the person presenting the statement and for all who listened. One sentence in particular stood out to me as a beacon, welcoming me into the harbor of peace that was unfortunately about to be drained dry just a few minutes later.

While Kay Woodcock was presenting her victim impact statement, she paused, then said, "Lori, Todd forgives you. I wanted to make sure you know that."

That struck me as a powerful invitation to peace. Todd is the biological father of J.J. He loved his son but had to give up parenting him due to his and J.J.'s mother's drug abuse. I don't personally know Todd, nor anything about his situation in life, but I imagine him basking in a state of peace as it pertains to Lori, while I am still lost in my anger. I realized right away that Todd is much further down the road to healing than I.

The whole experience of that day, characterized by the victim impact statements resulted in hope. Hope for healing from this awful crisis was underscored by the tremendous love that was shared and received among the majority of participants.

In stark contrast to the healing emotions provided by the victim impact statements, was Lori's statement. It was arrogant, condescending, self-absorbed, fictitious, evil, and many other descriptions that still fail to fully describe it. Judging from both the immediate and the ongoing reactions from all who heard it, the results included a tsunami of bitter and incredulous pain.

Standing before the crowded courtroom, Lori gave a bizarre and deranged speech lasting eight and a half minutes. She started by saying the following:

"I would like to start by quoting John from the New Testament in the Bible in John chapter 8, verse 7. Jesus says, "He that is without sin among you, let him first cast a stone at her. Then in the first verse of chapter 15, Jesus says, "Ye judge after the flesh, I judge no man. And yet if I judge, my judgment is true. Jesus knows me, and Jesus understands me. I mourn with all of you who mourn my children and Tammy. Accidental deaths happen. Suicides happen. Fatal side effects from medications happen."

She went on to describe how she died giving birth to Tylee, only to be sent back to complete her God-given mission. She claimed to talk to people in Heaven, where she wished desperately to return to.

Near the end of her statement, she said the following about the children she had been convicted for murdering:

"One of the times that Tylee came to me as a spirit after she died, she said – she commanded me – and she said to me: "Stop worrying, Mom. We are fine."

She knows how I worry and how I miss her.

The first time J.J. visited me after he passed away, he put his arm around me and he said to me: "You didn't do anything wrong, Mom. I love you, and I know you loved me every minute of my life."

J.J. Joshua Jackson was an adult spirit, and he was very, very tall when he put his arm around me. He is busy. He is engaged. He has jobs that he does there, and he is happy where he is. His life was short, but J.J.'s life was meaningful. J.J. was a wonderful person and touched the lives of everyone and I adored him every minute of his life."

Every other sentence I've left out sounded just as insane.

The countless lingering questions from her statement include: did she actually believe what she was spewing? And how can she be so far out of touch from reality? Debate on these topics continues. I believe some observations of how we all naturally experience this life provides a lot of insights and even answers to these perplexing questions and this frustrating affront to our senses and sensibilities. I believe those insights may bring more hope and more healing.

Lori started down her path the same way all of us do when we try to justify decisions in our lives that go against our conscience. My personal go-to violation of conscience example involves Blue

Bell Homemade Vanilla ice cream. I know, I know, it's not nearly as serious of a topic as what we've discussed so far. But maybe that levity is needed? Maybe by looking at a more mundane example, we can take a break from the mental load imposed by Lori's real actions.

I don't have any Blue Bell in my home, nor is it sold in my residence state. But when I am confronted with it, I usually eat as much of it as is available. Even though I barely cheated death a few years ago, narrowly surviving a heart attack caused by a clogged artery, I don't refuse the tempting Blue Bell that, in all likelihood, contributed to that nearly fatal event.

Here is where my decision-making relates to Lori's, and to most all of ours. In the moment of decision, my conscience impassionedly communicates to me that the Blue Bell will add another layer of cholesterol to my arteries. My impulses immediately respond with the rational lie that I programmed into myself long ago. They tell me that since I work out two hours per day, I don't have to worry about my heart and can go ahead and indulge in the well-earned Blue Bell treat.

When I initially chose to "rationalize" with that "rational lie," I knew that my exercise didn't negate the cholesterol. Sure, the exercise makes my heart muscle stronger, but it doesn't stop the cholesterol from clogging the pipes, which was the cause of the incident in the first place. In other words, I knew I was lying to myself, but that didn't stop me from building in certain preprogrammed responses that would help me ignore my conscience and let my appetites and impulses win this battle whenever it arises.

Why do I do this? Simple. I want the temporary pleasure of the Blue Bell more than I want the long-term health benefit of passing it up. It was only natural to realize that I go through the exact same routine for all my favorite sins and weaknesses.

As I started to pay attention more in my daily life, I realized that others are probably doing the same thing. And it's not only with eating decisions; it happens with every decision we make that flies in the face of our conscience's efforts to point out the obvious negative consequences of doing so.

Now, I am not completely without discipline in all decisions in my life, and neither are you. I believe most people are disciplined in most areas of our lives. Discipline just means that we allow our conscience to set healthy boundaries for most decisions. When you think about it, our conscience is the only barrier to the natural part of ourselves taking over our lives and running amuck.

Enter Lori's story of running amuck in the worst conceivable way. Please note that it's the natural process – which life allows – that she followed to get to a point to commit the most inconceivably wicked act that most of us can imagine – that of murdering her own children.

Lori, like all of us, has the fears, ego, appetites, and reasoning that serve as natural internal motivators as part of our daily decision making. That's a lot of factors to consider, and each one might be part of any decision a person makes. As such, trying to analyze or explain what goes into any one decision is probably too complex for us to be completely accurate, especially in such an extreme case as this. So, to characterize Lori's path we must over-simplify and speculate.

Let's speculate that Lori's ego really encouraged her to be someone extraordinary in life. Maybe her childhood, three failed marriages (to this point), and her self-perception of not standing out enough in life wasn't providing enough to satisfy that ego. Competing in the Mrs. Texas pageant and appearing on TV game shows may have given boosts to that ego, but those boosts were temporary at best.

She *did* know that one area in which she could excel and be recognized was her role as a mother. She had three children, including Colby from her second marriage, Tylee from her third marriage, and J.J. from her fourth. J.J. was her husband's great-nephew, whom they adopted when the parents were forced to give him up as they struggled with drug problems, so being a mother to him must have been especially lionizing.

Especially during this time of Lori and Charles' marriage, everyone on record who had insight into Lori and Charles' family described them as conscientious parents, specifically characterizing Lori as a great Mom.

Now, Lori has not only been revealed to have been an adulteress, she has more importantly received the maximum possible sentences for murdering the two youngest of those children and desecrating their bodies before having them abandoned in a pet cemetery; it causes somewhat of a public uproar to suggest she was a great mom in that new context. The uproar is often accompanied with people claiming someone who committed such horrific crimes must have always been evil in her heart, that she couldn't possibly have ever been a good mother. Perhaps that's true, but since none of us has seen into that heart at any time, that will continue endlessly as an unsolved debate. Here is my take on it:

Conceding that her heart (not nearly as clogged with Blue Bell ice cream as mine, by the way), at some undetermined point, was evil, there is still an explanation for this disparity. Those of us who know Lori, who spent time in her home with her and her children, and who witnessed how she interacted with them and spoke about them may have a valid perspective based on what we observed and experienced. Without seeing into her heart, all of our descriptions include how she was consistently patient, caring, loving, protecting, and selfless for her children.

Was this all an exhaustive, daily effort to feed her ego and hide the evil in her heart, an effort that eventually caused her to snap and overreact in the worst way? Maybe. Or it could also be the all-too natural process of life. It could be that Lori consistently chose to make the smaller decisions to ignore the only moderator to her natural self: her conscience.

Unchecked, our ego, appetites, and impulses demand that we exert more and more self-control as those impulses approach and embrace evil. Our conscience is the only protection we have from digressing to evil, whatever form evil is presently taking for us. No matter how you define evil, or what you believe its source to be, our society doesn't accept, condone, or excuse evil to the magnitude that it allows innocent people, especially children, to be murdered.

So, I'll state it this way: Lori demonstrated all of the actions by which most people define a "great mom" until she digressed on the path to becoming evil.

To become that evil, Lori had to overcome a great deal of "cognitive dissonance" – the internal struggle that accompanies each decision to pursue an act against the better judgment of her conscience. It works that way for all of us. A common way to overcome that is to create a fantasy that rationalizes the action, just as I did with my Blue Bell ice cream decision. As more and more decisions associated with the original fantasy have to be made, the fantasy grows into very deluded thinking. That is an oversimplification of how alternative realities are created, of course; each time Lori decided to ignore her conscience in order to allow for the ever-increasing demands of her natural self – her ego, in this speculative examination – added to the alternative realities that she continually had to expand to accommodate those demands.

Now add the external influences that affected those decisions: family dynamics, friends' influences, religious experiences, societal norms, good and/or evil influences, and many more sources can all play a part in this ever-increasingly complex dynamic of decision-making.

Note that these many external influences are just that, external. Influences can play a part in decision-making, but only at the invitation of the decision-maker. That is how nature, or natural law, holds the decision-maker responsible for the decisions. In nature, there is no allowable excuse that "the devil made me do it," or that "it was justified because God told me to do it." That is as true for all of us as it is for Lori and her co-conspirators Chad and Alex. We are accountable for our actions. Those three are accountable for their murders.

Did Lori believe the refuse she was spewing during the sentencing? I believe she did because she has barricaded herself safely inside her carefully crafted and heinous alternative reality. While she creates and revises that reality, she must at some level be aware that the decisions going into it are evil to begin with. But once they become part of the alternative reality, she commits herself to them completely as her new "truth."

So, her deluded version of reality becomes a self-protection mechanism for the person who made the conscious decisions to override the conscience. The protection is only effective against the pain caused by the internal struggle. It serves as no protection from the consequences of the actions taken.

Can you imagine if Lori, for whatever unlikely reason, emerged from the evil, complex alternative reality she created along with her co-conspirators? She would have to face the unfathomable pain that is the natural result of having perpetrated the evil of murdering her children and others in order to satisfy her own pathetic, self-serving desires. We oversimplified those desires for this explanation; it was probably a complex combination of meaningless, self-serving motives. Regardless, the pain would undoubtedly be more than a human could bear.

This is my attempt to explain how someone that many of us described, at one point in time, as a great mom, could digress so unimaginably far so fast. And, I believe, it provides a logical explanation as to how Lori could believe what she was spewing at the sentencing. It's the same path that we all follow when we want something our conscience advises against. Fortunately, most of us choose to allow our conscience to draw a line long before it digresses so far. But it's the same natural path on which we all travel.

It's the only way that makes sense to me so far. It is also my best attempt to find answers by following natural law. These explanations are certainly not more valid than yours or anyone else's explanations for these tragedies. Until the actual answers to all our questions come from the sources of the actions – and neither Lori nor Chad may ever reveal their true intentions to us – I believe the best we can do is to share our ideas, our healing, and our attempts to understand such a dark, dark mystery together.

CHAPTER TWELVE: Support Systems

Adam

A friend of mine (who I'm going to keep anonymous) recently reached out to me. "I was watching a Netflix documentary on cults the other day," he said, "and I saw your face, Adam! I yelled out in my house, watching TV in my living room, 'I know him! What the hell happened?'" Then, seeming a little embarrassed, he stopped himself and said, "Sorry, I forgot to ask if you were okay." We both laughed, and I explained that this had become my new normal recently, so I was used to it.

Unfortunately, his reason for calling – and for watching that documentary in the first place – wasn't nearly as amusing. His wife, he explained, had 'freaked out' and joined some weird cult recently, prompting him to research information on cults in general. That led him to the documentary, and the documentary led him to me.

We talked for about two hours. My friend told me about his wife, about how she met some crazy lady who'd taught her crazy things and had her living her life in a crazy way. He didn't get into all the specifics, but he was asking for help. So, he started by asking me all kinds of questions about what happened with Lori and Alex, and if Chad was a cult leader. I told him what I thought, but explained that I didn't have all the answers.

Then he started asking for advice., "Every time I try to get someone in my family or her family to help her," he explained, "nobody wants to get into the middle of it. I can't go to the police, but I'm afraid to leave my kids with her. I'm scared she will kill them."

It broke my heart to hear that – especially given how much it resonated with my experience. I told him as much, about how I went through a similar experience trying to get Lori help. About how my family cut me off. About how the police didn't do anything when Charles was telling them Lori had threatened to kill him.

My friend wanted to do an intervention with his wife, but nobody wanted to help him or get in the middle of it. He was asking me what to do, and as much as I could relate, I couldn't give him any answers.

My friend hung up the phone, distraught and helpless not knowing what to do. And for all my experience dealing with the exact same thing, I was left still asking the same question: what do you do if someone you love drastically changes their behaviors but hasn't done anything against the law yet? It seems obvious that society needs a way to help people who are headed for the deep end before they get there, but how? Could I have done more? Could I have held an intervention despite the lack of support from the rest of my family? Or would Lori and Alex have just tried to kill me if I'd cornered them like that?

Frustration and loneliness reign supreme when you're on one side of a debate while everyone else is on the other side – especially when you can see things they just can't. Standing alone can be hard. Hard enough to make you question what you're even trying to do in the first place. Thoughts of self-doubt constantly ran through my head. Should I have just gone along with my family, cut Charles off, and given Lori a pass? My family wouldn't have cut me off, and I wouldn't have been so lonely. On the other hand, I *knew* they were wrong. I *knew* Lori, Alex, and Chad were plunging toward something truly dangerous, and I wouldn't have just *stopped* knowing by giving up and falling in line. It was almost insurmountable, making that decision, but at the end of the day, I just couldn't let Charles try to handle the situation by himself. I needed to try to help him.

At the end of the day, I guess that's what it comes down to. You have to stand up for what *you* know is right, even if it's difficult, even if it means standing alone facing everyone else. I still don't know what I could have done differently, or if there even *was* anything I could have done that would have worked. I do know one thing, though. If I could have seen Charles one more time before he was killed, I would have hugged him and told him how brave he was for trying to get Lori help. I would tell him that I knew he loved Lori, that I knew that the only thing he wanted was to get his old

Lori back. Other than that, I'm not sure I would have changed a thing.

***

There is one big thing me and my son Zac can be grateful for: we didn't get killed. We survived the 'zombie hunt' that Chad, Lori, and Alex went on that claimed the lives of others. But sometimes that feels like small comfort. Zac and I have been through so much in the past 5 years that I sometimes struggle to believe that we are actually still moving forward. Each new revelation about Lori, Chad, and Alex's actions was earth shattering for us – first about what they did to Charles, then what they did to the kids. We have talked and tried to support each other, but it has been truly unbearable at times. I'm filled with so much sorrow, not just for the people who were killed but the survivors who have to live through this.

I feel for Zac especially. I love my son so much, and it kills me to see him so hurt and sad. I'm sure other parents reading this will sympathize with me when I say that I would do anything to take away all of my child's pain and sorrow if I could. Zac has had his heart broken and smashed to pieces. He loved Charles and Tylee and J.J. Of course, I also loved Alex and Lori and had a great relationship with both of them. But think about it for a second: you're 18, 19, or 20 years old and trying to absorb everything that has happened. Lori and Alex, the uncle and aunt he loved, killed his uncle Charles and his cousins Tylee and J.J. On top of all that, in the middle of this shit storm, his own grandma, grandpa, and his other aunt turned their back on him. The family that Zac has known his whole life, the one he loved absolutely, turned their back to him and cut him off.

Zac had a loving and special relationship with everyone in my family. He helped everyone when he could, made them all laugh, and constantly told them how much he loved them. He was a devoted cousin to Tylee and J.J. and spent so much quality time with them.

He even helped teach Tylee to drive. He called me one day when he lived with Lori, and he and Tylee were out to get food at a drive-in. They were on Bluetooth – Zac was talking, and Tylee was driving. I said, "Tylee, make sure you're going the speed limit. You don't want a ticket before you get your license." Zac started laughing, and Tylee said, "What is the speed limit here?" Zac was joking and said 35 MPH. Tylee screamed, "I'm going 50!!! " We all started to laugh.

Zac watched J.J. a bunch too while staying at Lori's house and felt a deep love for him. They developed a close relationship where J.J. would always get Zac to play with him.

Zac also adored my mom. He called her Mimi. The two of them would talk almost every day about anything and everything. My mom has a love for sports – well, mostly football and basketball, just like Zac. He would talk with her for hours about NFL and NBA players and teams on the regular. Zac told Mimi everything, and Mimi told Zac everything. There was a love that was deep and a bond that was unbreakable. At least, it was supposed to be. But when Charles was shot and killed, it started a family revolution. You've already read about the enormous family fight we had at my mom's house, so I won't recount it here. Needless to say, it created an enormous rift not only between me and my parents, but between them and Zac as well.

During the whole screaming match, Zac was trying to tell my mom something that Lori said previously. She was *not* having it. He tried to tell my mom about something sexually inappropriate that Lori had said. My mom, of course, claimed that Lori never would have said something like that to Zac. Lori was supposed to be more spiritual than anyone in the family. She even got rid of cable TV because she didn't want any bad things in her house.

I said, "Mom, Zac wouldn't lie about that. He has no reason to lie – think about it." All the while, Zac just had this crushed look on his face as he looked at the grandma that he so loved and adored calling him a liar and shutting him off. She was just too far gone under the little spell Lori seemed to cast on people.

My mom crushed Zac that night. The two of them haven't spoken to each other since – even three or four years after the fight happened. Zac wants nothing to do with her, my dad, or my sister Summer, because they all believed Lori and didn't listen to him or me. So now, instead of just losing two uncles and two cousins, Zac has also lost a grandma, a grandpa, and two aunts. He doesn't want anything to do with my family, and I can't say I blame him. I told him he had the right to feel however he wanted to feel, and that I would always support him and put him first in my life over anyone.

126

I did tell him that *I* have to forgive; otherwise, the anger and hurt would just eat me alive. So, I have forgiven my mom and dad and Summer, and I'm trying to build back a relationship with my family at large. Zac is not ready to do that, and he may never be ready to do that. I'm okay with whatever he decides to do. Nobody can judge him because nobody has walked in his shoes. We will see what ends up happening with our family, but at least Zac can know that I'll have his back no matter what.

But he and I have plenty on our plates regardless of what happens with the family. I've been pondering for a while now if Zac and I will ever get back to our old selves. I think I'm starting to see the beginning of that kind of healing. I recently moved back to Arizona from St. George to be closer to my son. Zac and I love going to the movies. We even enjoy watching the trailers; we'll put our thumbs up if we want to see it and down if we don't. Then, when the movie gets going, we will joke around and talk about scenes in the movie we could do spoofs for. There have been times when watching a movie at the theater, we would laugh so hard that we would cry and not be able to stop. If anyone reading this has ever been in a movie theater with us, I apologize profusely.

It's fortunate that Zac and I have a lot to bond over. First off, we look alike and have similar demeanors – we both try to be peacemakers at the very least. We also love sports, and we love our friends. Since I have moved back to Arizona, I have made an attempt to go to Zac's gym and work out with him every morning. I feel so happy every time I do. I get to start my day off by seeing my only son. We've even developed a routine: we do cardio first thing, then do weights, then play basketball, and then we end with ten to fifteen minutes in the sauna. I still look forward to spending time with him. He is literally the best kid in the world. I know most of you think that about your kid, but when other parents tell you how great your kid is, it's the honest truth. I know he is not a kid anymore – he's already 24 – but I have so many great memories of Zac from when he was younger that he'll always be my kid in my mind.

I remember when Zac was 10 – or maybe 11 or 12; I can't remember – and I coached his flag football team in Arizona. It was when Zac was first starting to form his love of sports. I coached him in both football and basketball, which were his favorites. It was such a thrill for me to watch Zac grow as an athlete. Something that stood out one day at practice, Zac said, "Coach, can we do this play?" Everyone on the team knew I was his dad, but he didn't want any special privileges, so he started calling me coach like the rest of the players.

I feel like I'm rambling, but maybe that's the point. Despite everything that's happened, I still have my son. We still have each other. And whatever else happens, however long it takes us to bounce back from this tragedy, we'll have each other's backs the entire way.

CHAPTER THIRTEEN: Silver Linings (Words from Our Community)

Rex

Before we ever started work on this book, Adam and I started our own podcast series: Tylee and J.J.'s Silver Linings. While we had originally only ever planned ten episodes, the community that formed around it and the things they shared with us prompted us to continue to this day. This book is meant to stand on its own and provide the totality of our insights into the tragedy our family has experienced, but at the same time, it felt wrong not to acknowledge the place and community that propelled us to a place where we felt inspired to share what we have to say. So, Adam and I have selected comments from our community and included them here, along with our thoughts on them.

Note that we have anonymized the usernames of the commenters whose statements we've included here. Though everything was posted to a public forum, we still felt it best to play it on the safe side in regard to this.

Now, let's hear from our listeners.

ABOUT THE PODCAST

The purposes of the podcasts have evolved since its origin, and we evolved with them.

Our initial purpose was to share family perspectives on the murders of the victims to those interested. Reactions to those perspectives, we felt, would give us valuable input for this book. We believe both those purposes were fulfilled.

As I said, we started with the idea of just doing 10 episodes of the podcast. We estimated that that would be all of the family perspective needed, which turned out to be a pretty accurate projection. We could have stopped at that point. However, we realized that there were many more purposes being achieved by the podcast.

The first episode had more than 60,000 views just on YouTube. We had been warned by our YouTube mentors, Lauren Matthias and Gigi Makelvey, that we were not prepared for the amount of interest there would be in our podcasts. They were right! There were more than 1,400 comments on that first episode. We tried to read them all, but there just wasn't time.

The comments were overwhelmingly positive and supportive. However, human nature, or at least our nature, seems to focus on those comments that are negative.

"Making a quick buck and getting "famous" on such horrific murders."

"Two used car salesman types attempting to profit from horrific tragedy."

"Too simplistic. Hard to listen to. I hope this gives you, the hosts, the process you need to put your hurt somewhere that helps you to live your lives well. As for silver linings ... I get that there has to be a positive spin to entice an audience, but no silver linings here. Except maybe some will stop making their life choices based on bullshit books other ppl write."

"This feels gross and wrong. the name of the pod is weird. You guys probably hadn't seen those kids in years, now you want to make a whole podcast dedicated to talking about how your sick sister tortured and killed her kids? You guys are related to Lori and that gives me the ick, and now you're making money off these poor kids name too. I can't wait for Chad's trial to be done so we can start to move on from this case. Let the real loved ones of those kids grieve."

"Bunch of grifters Adam you abandoned Charles that day trying to cash in on this tragedy your families usual MO."

Mean-spirited comments do hurt, but I quickly developed a perspective that served me well. To me, these people are involved in the same cause as us. There is only one side in this tragedy – we all want justice for the victims – especially for J.J., Tylee, Charles, and Tammy! The people who make these negative comments are saying, in my mind, "We want justice for the victims. We don't trust your motives in this. You want something else; money, fame, or whatever." I can understand others questioning my motives. I choose to interpret their passion as energy toward a common goal. I'll take that.

The source of the most caustic comments was our perceived motive of doing the podcast and writing a book to make money from the death of relatives, as seen in the preceding examples. If it weren't so mean-spirited, it could be comical to us. The obvious response which we never really did use was to state, "Anyone who thinks that you can make money with infrequent podcasts and writing a book have neither started podcasting, nor have written a book." To address this particular topic, we posted a "Response."

The Responses were started for addressing specific topics that would not take an entire podcast episode to address. In addition to the topic of our money motive, we posted Responses on the topics of Lori & Alex's relationship, Joseph Ryan, Melani, Stacey, and other family members early on.

Responses are also a way to acknowledge commonly requested topics when we don't have much to offer, or to clear up a difference of perception. Adam and I very much value perspectives which are different from ours. We don't mind people questioning our statements, our actions, or our perspectives. We don't mind tough questions, since we believe we all just want the truth. We especially appreciate when people ask in a straight-forward manner without being accusational, such as:

> Commenter 1:
>
> *Adam can you explained what happened the morning Charles was killed. Apparently, you had texted with him and found out Alex was at Lori's. You were "very worried" about Charles going in the house. Then you couldn't reach Charles again. Next thing, according to foia/media and your own words, you left town with your son to go to a friends home and expressed your concern about Charles to him. He then googled Charles name and found out he was dead days later. I have been completely confused about your actions that day and a few days after. Please help us understand.*

This earnest and respectfully posed question about Adam's actions around Charles being shot was a hot topic. We had no idea. Not having been on social media during this time, neither of us had known of the ignorant accusations made against Adam due to a lack of information. Many people were, and some remain to this day, ignorantly caustic about this toward Adam. This required a full podcast to address. We addressed it in our 5th episode.

As we were approaching the tenth podcast episode, we realized we had provided about as much family perspective as possible for us without completely violating relationships inside the family. Many of our family members were not supportive of our podcasts. In their expressed views, whether to us or to others in the family, we had gone too far by even beginning to invite the entire outside world into our family through the podcasts. We could have stopped the podcast with a feeling of accomplishment. But many other dynamics had come into play.

There's another reason we continue to do the podcast in spite of the vitriol surrounding it. Even though the number of views and comments had reduced by half from the early episodes, those comments were rather compelling. As we had continued to honestly share ourselves and the dynamics of our healing from these horrific tragedies, our subscribers started doing the same. Their expressions of love and support were genuine and brought unexpected healing. And the healing was not just for us; there were overwhelming comments on how much healing, comfort, and understanding this new "community" was providing to those who listened and commented.

While we continue to acknowledge the obvious fact that we aren't therapists and are not pretending to provide any professional services, it seems that people love to share in the compelling realities of life's tragedies. And, judging by the many comments, we *all* have them. We don't have them all the time, but they stay with us and provide a small amount of understanding which we can offer to others when they are enduring the seemingly impossible burdens of life we each endure at times.

When there is so much love, healing, and support being provided by, and to so many people, how do we walk away from providing that through the podcast? The eight to ten thousand people per week who continue to participate in the podcasts is a lot of people. Reading their comments of love, support, and sharing their stories is too compelling for Adam and me to just walk away from.

We also realize that there is much more of the tragedy from Lori and her co-conspirators yet to unfold. There is potentially much more for us to contribute by pursuing the many unanswered questions yet to be addressed.

FROM OUR OPTIMISTS

The subscribers to our podcast wanted a name to go by. Apparently, that is a common practice in the podcast world. We asked for suggestions, and they poured in, to include the following (presented as received):

- *metallic lusters*
- *"Soul Searchers"*
- *"SEEKERS"*
- *We all should be your Angel's Adam & Gruncle Rex's Angels's*
- *"Path Finders" or the "Truth Finders."*
- *"SHINERS" meaning: someone that reflects light (our goal); people rubbing tarnish off of silver (our process); slang for a black eye (the hard knocks of life, our struggles)*

- *Silvers*
- *Liners*
- *Silver Soldiers*
- *Silver Linings and Silverados*
- *Silver Linings and the Silversmiths*
- *Gruncle Groupies*
- *FRIENDS!*
- *THE IMPECCABILES*
- *"charms"*
- *Every CLOUD, has a Silver Lining. The CLOUDS*
- *The Silver Liners*
- *Truth Seekers*

We love the creativity and the many suggestions. While we appreciated each option presented to us, we eventually settled on calling our subscribers "Optimists." Here was the suggestion from Commenter 2:

Rex and Adam - I've been thinking about a nickname for us, your subscribers, and something I thought of was "Optimists!" My thinking is, A silver lining is a metaphor for optimism in our society/culture/the US/the World. And that means a negative occurrence may have a positive aspect to it. Or that good can come from bad! So if you, Rex and Adam, are discussing Silver Linings, then you both are optimists and so are all those who subscribe!! Optimists subscribe to an overall philosophy that good/positivity/success/ healing/greater knowledge & understanding can triumph over evil/pain/difficulty! Though it can take mental effort. We have to seek the good that can come from bad, and those who do that are Optimists!!

We love our Optimists!

After all, they're what kept us going. After the original ten episodes that we had planned, we received so many comments about how much healing is taking place among the community, including Adam's and my healing that we felt we just had to keep going. Here are a just a few of many, many of the compelling, heartfelt sentiments we were sent by the Optimists:

Commenter 3:

For Adam, I saw a lot of frustration tension and stress along with deep sorrow, grief, which is all very understandable! That level of tension seems to have gone down. You seem a lot happier. I think the affirmations that all of us have giving you and Rex in the comments have probably been a huge measure of healing. Plus, being able to talk about all of this so openly is truly like a therapy session. Although your original topic was a strange and very odd Downer, I always loved and eagerly anticipated seeing a new video of yours. Please don't ever worry about them being too long. I could listen to you two for a couple of hours easily! So glad you got to do your first live tonight gentleman! Great job to both of you!

Commenter 4:

Adam and Rex, I so appreciate all you're doing. You two are working towards healing as well as helping us (who didn't know J.J., Tylee, Charles or Tammy) with the closure I've needed since following this case from day one.

Commenter 5:

In the past, I had a situation with my adult brother who is/was the most sensitive, thoughtful guy who went through a major personality change, put himself in dangerous situations with dangerous people mainly because he trusted blindly (English wasn't his first language he relocated to America at around 15 years old). Once he turned 18-19 he wanted independence and I helped him, get a job, get an apartment and furnishings. I even purchased a really nice truck that I hoped to give him for his birthday. However, I noticed he was struggling mentally and emotionally, it started effecting his life in the worst ways. I tried everything to reach him realizing he needed professional help. We talked and he agreed to go to a doctor and I went with him to help explain what was happening. I loved him and wanted to help him but the doctor wouldn't communicate with me at all due to his privacy. He decided he didn't want or need help and I watched as his world crashed down around him, helpless. I went everywhere to try to get someone that would listen to me that could help him because I know he's a really good person and basically everyone said he's an adult it's up to him if he doesn't want to get help then there's nothing you can do about it. I couldn't find anyone to listen or help, basically, everyone said I was being codependent or enabling his situation by wanting to help him. It was one of the most frustrating experiences that ended up with me having zero contact with him now basically due to him being an adult and I couldn't find any one after 8 years of trying anything and everything to get him help. When I saw Charles Vallow begging the police for help with Laurie it brought back so many memories and unresolved feelings. It truly makes me cry watching that video of Charles begging, and there's nothing he can do. From what I've heard my brothers life went from bad to worse. He really went downhill. He had children and he doesn't have custody of them. It's horrible because he had an amazing childhood and loving mother and father that passed away when he was 15. Anyway, long story short I was wondering if you could do a show or find someone that would know what people should do in situations where you know someone really truly has changed and they're not being realistic... Where do you go? What can you do?

These kinds of thoughts and stories shared by so many people helped us to realize what this community was becoming. It was a safe place to share what people may not have shared before. In the case of Commenter 5, she shared her story after many comments being incredibly supportive of us and of other Optimists. Then, she got the chance to share the words above. It's a beautiful opportunity to have a place where we can all help bear one another's burdens!

So many of our Optimists "have our back" when the occasional troll strikes. Because of that, the number of trolls commenting has significantly decreased over time. Here is a common sentiment we read:

Commenter 6:

People have such nerve, i'm so sick of hearing you guys having to explain yourselves to people in the comments all the time. I know people have the right as you said, to feel the way they do but I wish some people would be aware of the line that exist between people that are not close to you. Shit is just rude. IDK how else to explain it. . . . Knowing your energy, as much as a viewer/stranger can pick up on, I would never imagine that either of you somehow made a huge mistake in the past as far as one of the cases go and if you did it would have been worked out or at least addressed by yourselves or the cops. It's nobody's right to ask these things of you. . I'm so sorry you have to see these comments I'm sure there are worse ones that you don't mention. I want so bad for you to get thru these early days of closure even tho Charles' case is coming up. . . .I know I probably sound dumb or whatever, I'm just speaking from a place of genuine concern and love. Love for each person I meet or see that have beautiful hearts and spirits - + concern for your heart, your healing + what the road in front of you looks like. I'm so glad you guys are continuing with the podcast! Thanks for that, + for whatever pains(if any) you guys have to deal with in your own lives as a result. It's super cool that you both not only recognize the curiosity + the interest but that you were on board to take it further with the podcast. Just wanted to say thanks and to show my support , and respect

We always get a grateful laugh from people's support! As a practice, we don't delete all negative comments, nor do we block very many trolls from doing so in the first place. In fact, in the more than 4,000 comments to date, less than 2% of which have been negative, we have deleted less than two dozen comments, and have blocked only three people. Those people were just mean-spirited!

This generous Optimist's question gave us the opportunity to express our thoughts on the subject of trolls during a short response episode we posted:

Commenter 7:

I love you both so much and I can't even imagine the pain, sadness, anger, confusion and betrayal you have felt. I love how easy going you are Grunkle Rex so I have a question for you. Both you and Adam have said that everyone is entitled to their own opinions and feelings, but is there 1 thing that makes you really angry that someone has had a difference of opinion about (with the case) from you? Like you can't even understand why someone would feel/think that way? Just curious

I answered this by confessing there are basically two categories of perspectives with which I choose not to deal.

I feel just a little protective of Adam. When the same person continues to question his actions the day of and after Charles was killed, or tries to throw a past tragedy from his radio life in his face, that is purely born out of ignorant vile. Those topics have been addressed many times. When they come up, we reference what we have already said so anyone can listen to an explanation, but if they persist, we just block them because we don't feel the need to engage further.

Similarly, when people persist in obviously just being mean-spirited about a topic, such as religion, mistaken conclusions about family members' past, other Optimists' comments, or our financial motives for the podcasts, we won't engage. The rule we follow goes something like, "Don't wrestle with a pig. You only get covered in filth, and the pig enjoys it!"

So, the miracle that seems to be happening with the podcast, which we can't quite explain, is the healing that is happening with so many of the Optimists – again, including me and Adam. We love the community interaction that happens when Optimists comment on other Optimists' posts to offer encouragement.

Commenter 8:

I rewatching / relistening and can relate to Rex, i feel so touched by his tears. After I lost my husband I cryed around 5 years..Its so touching Rex, I also dont want loose my feelings / feel. Im not totally healed after many years now but its more like things can happen ,be more grateful, listen ,bring and show share love to others

Responses to Commenter 8:

I totally understand. We are never completely healed. We grieve and move forward. It's one step at a time. Sometimes it's a step forward and sometimes it's a step backwards.

Commenter 9:

Praise Jesus! You guys made a new podcast. I'm trying to kick my addictions (1 major, 2 minor none of them good for me) and I've been going through it. I even asked God, what he wanted from me. I finished doing laundry and here are you 2 wonderful men, saying such kind words for all of us. I feel like it was telling me to hold on and keep going. And the support I've received from others when I shared a little bit a couple of weeks ago. You all are my people. If you don't think you're helping anyone or only a few, you're helping more then you think. Love and kindness are powerful! Thank you.

Responses to Commenter 9:
Hang in there lady and stick to your recovery one day at a time. You are not alone. I am praying for you

and:
Keep fighting that battle!! Been down that rabbit hole and it's tough!! Support is here in this community

Commenter 10:
I'm 68 on the 18th this month, and from my young perspective I am coming to understand that my life is a series of healings. I agree that I never heal, I just Integrate my life experiences or I don't. I am blessed when I am able to realize that I know absolutely nothing and I am actually fine with that. I just try to live my life one day at a time, stay in the moment and stay on my own side of the street, which means mind my own business and stay out of judgment which is almost a full time job! I so adore the two of you... just ballbusting right into everything that's happened in your

lives, with such humility and honest feelings, which gives me such HOPE for my future. We all have regrets when we don't listen to our guts, but there's plenty that beats us down everyday, I don't need to add more to that situation. God Bless.

The search for answers and healing will continue. It's great to be part of a wonderfully supportive community in that search!

THOUGHTS FROM ADAM

Engaging with the Optimists and reading their comments has absolutely been a silver lining for me and Rex over the past four months since starting our podcast. Here are some comments we've received that particularly resonated with me, and some words from myself about what I learned from them.

Commenter 11:
Here is my 2 cents on this podcast. love the subject of todays podcast, by the way. So, my oldest son had an issue with pills/drugs for a while and 1 learned something interesting while attending his meetings. One of his counselors told us that addicts have flipped the process of thinking. Normally we have top down thinking. meaning when we want something like chokolade, immediately our mind goes into work and says things like... It's too late for that or its not

good for you. But with an addict, that never happens They have what they call caveman thinking, which is the lower part of you brain that controls you main needs like food, sex and other main needs. So, to an addict, they feel a need and it has to be fulfilled! But, how do you get to flip your thinking like that?? answer is, by allowing your body to control you! They live in a ME world where everything is about them and what they want. Can you change it back to a normal way of thinking? Yes. When we fast, we deny our body of food and water and we have to keep telling our body NO. When we take control of our desires and appetites, we control our brain also. The more we practice that, the stronger we get. I'm sure everyone started out with a top down thinking, but over time, as we give into our body, time and time again things change In the case of Lori, it has beer mentioned that Lori always got what she wanted. So, if Lori was never told NO, she is being trained to live in a ME world, her way, her needs are always more important, and over time you create a narcissist and they have caveman thinking My ex husband woke up every night around 2 or 3 am hungry. He would then get up and eat a peanut butter sandwich and drink a big glass of chocolate milk,. He would then complain of lack of sleep and about gaining weight. When I told him to stop feeding his body at night, because he was training his body to wake up then, he looked at me funny and said NO WAY. If his body wanted something, he would give it to it!! That example is of course not a crime to do, but what happens when a person like that wants someone elses spouse? Wants sex with a child or any thing else?? They get what they want, because they never learned to deny themselves of anything They don't even THINK of the consequences, because that would mean to deny themselves of something and that is not an option in their mind. You can also create narcissistic children by denying them their basic needs or need for love. If those needs are not meet, they become hyper focused on meeting their needs when grown and is only able to see their own needs. Anyways, I'm no professional, this is just my thoughts Learn to take control of your body, so the body don't control you!!

I read this comment after one of our broadcasts, and I was blown away. I've identified several points within it that I think anyone can learn from. I like comments that make intuitive sense to me, and she hit each topic she brought up square on the head. I know how important fasting is for the body, but also for the brain. I love the analogy she used about her husband eating a peanut butter and jelly sandwich and chocolate milk in the middle of the night. The decision is to make his hunger pains go away so he can sleep, and the consequence of that action is weight gain. I love how she challenged him to stop engaging in the destructive behavior, and he said, "no way!" I also love that our podcast community feels safe enough with us that they are willing to share such personal stories.

She mentioned her son was addicted to pills, and that she went with him to one of his meetings. I think it's fantastic that she was able to learn so much from that experience, and I love even more that she felt comfortable sharing what she learned with the rest of our wonderful community. Learning – and bonding – is happening all the time with these folks.

Commenter 12:

So I am 59 years old and it has taken just until 1 ½ years ago to forgive the man that sa'ed me at the young age of 5-7yrs old. I knew inside me that He had been holding me back ALL my life. He changed what God put down here and for a reason. God blessed me with such a bright light deep down in my soul!!! God doesn't make mistakes!! He has been with me all my life, especially when I need him. So on the forgiving...I knew it was time and it SET ME FREE!! It took me 50 yrs to stop running from the dark thoughts and the monster not left behind...I am truly happy and joyous today. Yes forgiveness is essential I believe!

I love this comment because I also feel this way. During one of our recording sessions for the podcast, I remember telling Uncle Rex and our optimists that I needed to forgive to move on. I know some people say they just can't bring themselves to forgive, and I understand that sentiment. However, I feel like if I hold in the anger or disappointment, those feelings will just eat me up inside.

Forgiving is freeing for me and others. I'm glad that this woman who made this comment after over 50 years decided to forgive. Just think: if she could have done that sooner in life, she wouldn't have had to struggle so much with that. I know when someone offends you or does something terrible to you that your very first thought isn't forgiving. Doing sois a process and, fortunately, doesn't have a time limit in my opinion. I know that I, personally, have to go through several layers and process everything before I can truly forgive someone. I know everyone experiences this process differently, but I just know from experience that the sooner you can do it, the better off you will feel.

Commenter 13:
Way too much smiling while discussing such a tragedy from you both, especially Rex

Commenter 14:
I think this podcast/ YouTube show is top notch, I have the utmost respect for Adam and Rex

I decided to share these two different comments, both of which were posted on episode of the podcast, because they are completely different. I will address them in order.

For the first comment, Rex and I continue to invite people to be part of our podcast community whether they agree with us or not. We have always said that everyone has the right to their opinion. We just don't want people to be mean on purpose. The first comment says, "we are smiling too much." Rex and I don't really have extensive experience in dealing with tragedies. To put it bluntly, we don't know how to act. This is all new to us. I *can* tell you that dealing with what we have dealt with the last four years has been nothing if not overwhelming. We even have said on most episodes of our podcasts that we are trying to deal with many different emotions. We may laugh or use dark humor. Rex has cried on several podcasts. I have become incredibly angry and have gone off on tangents. We have displayed all kinds of emotions and reactions. Again, I said we don't want to judge anyone or have people judge us. Judging is such an easy thing to do; most of us probably need to work on that. Laughing and smiling is something I do instinctively, and that Rex does as well. This is just one of the ways we try to deal with our emotions.

The second comment was from an optimist who really appreciated our podcast. We have way more comments of support and love and appreciation for our podcast than we do detractors. I think this is the reason our podcast community feels like we are all friends and family. We love that our podcast can bring people together, and that we can support each other so consistently. The comment said they had respect for Rex and me. Well, I also have respect for our audience. Respect is something earned not given.

Commenter 15:

Mine is a long story. At 14 my 2 year old sister was murdered by my step mom. Child Abuse Homicide with insufficient evidence. 40 years later I am trying to find a lady named Laurie who knows what happened that day. I know from her EXACTLY what happened but that makes it hearsay. Praying everyday, talking to the original detective. Maybe if I start speaking the story, somebody will find her. All I know is Laurie moved to Arizona at 15 within a day of the murder. I have been living with the guilt for 45 years that I didn't take that little girl Jessica away. I confronted my step mom about the abuse, and didn't change a thing. All I could do at 14 was pick her up and take her away

After reading this comment, I started thinking about the last time I saw Tylee alive, and I'm filled with 'what ifs.' I think everyone has at least a couple moments like that, memories that make them think, "Well, what if I had done (blank)? Would that have made a difference? I'm sure there are people who will literally get away with murder in this life, but I believe everyone will be judged in heaven according to their works. I also believe that Jesus will judge everyone perfectly. I know sometimes we are hard on ourselves – I scold myself all the time. I have a friend, though, who said, "You need to learn how to give yourself grace." I now try to do just that any time I find myself being my own worst critic. In life, we all are given hard times, and existence itself can seem painful and unfair. We need to realize that we are not perfect, that we all are going to experience lapses in judgment, and that when we do, we need to give ourselves some grace.

I think that's the perfect note on which to end this segment. We will continue to have the backs of our listeners, and I sincerely hope they'll continue to support each other in the same way. From Rex and me both, thank you so much to everyone in our community. I hope you stick with us as we continue to navigate our way through healing and appreciate each and every silver lining that we can find.

THE END

Timeline

October 2018 - Lori Vallow and Chad Daybell meet at a conference for a radical doomsday group called Preparing a People. Chad was an author, and Lori had read several of his books related to the "last days," or the days preceding the prophesied Second Coming of Jesus Christ. Lori and others also revered Chad's supposed spiritual gifts. At the conference, Chad repeatedly told Lori that they had been married in a previous life.

End of October 2018 - Lori and Chad begin communicating electronically. According to a felony indictment, shortly after communications begin, Chad and Lori start discussing the "religious beliefs" that led them to justifying killing J.J. and Tylee, two of Lori's children who were still under her care. Soon after they begin communicating, they strike up an adulterous affair. At this time, Lori was married to Charles Vallow and living in Gilbert, AZ, while Chad was married to Tammy Daybell and living in Salem, Idaho (just outside of Rexburg).

October 30, 2018 - Chad Daybell emails Lori Vallow with "Family History Documents," including a ranking of her various family members based on a "light or dark spiritual scale." This kind of classification is an outgrowth of the extreme, fringe religious beliefs they both share.

December 5, 2018 - Chad and Lori make their first appearance together on the podcast "Time to Warrior Up," which was produced by "Preparing a People."

January 2019 - Chad and Lori exchange emails that describe their strange, concocted rationalization for killing "zombies" -- people who they claimed had been possessed by dark spirits. Their fantasy suggests that such evil spirits had replaced the spirits who originally inhabited the bodies, so those bodies must be killed to allow their original spirits to progress out of the limbo in which they were trapped. According to these emails, Lori and Chad believe Charles – and later Tylee, J.J., and Chad's wife, Tammy – to be zombies.

January 28 & 29, 2019 - Lori begins to transfer money from Charles' business accounts to different, still unknown accounts. Lori tells Charles that she was a "god" and was destined to help the 144,000 individuals prophesied to be saved during Christ's Second Coming. She also tells him that if he gets in the way of her mission, she will kill him.

January 30, 2019 - Lori calls Charles while he is away on a business trip. While communicating with him, Lori keeps referring to Charles as "Nick Schneider." When Charles asks who Nick Schneider is, she tells him that "Nick" was Charles' real name, because Nick had killed Charles and taken his identity. She mentions that she cannot trust Charles and that she will destroy him financially. Lori also repeatedly warns him that she will kill him upon his return home and that she had an angel there to help her dispose of the body.

January 31, 2019 - Lori cancels Charles' return trip and uses a spare key to move his truck to an undisclosed location. When Charles eventually returns home, he finds that all of his belongings are gone, and that his family is missing. Charles contacts the police for assistance, showing them a petition Charles already had in place for an involuntary hold for Lori at a mental health facility, Community Bridges. Lori willingly submits to be evaluated at Community Bridges and passes the exam with "flying colors."

February 2019 - At some point during the month, Lori Vallow disappears for 58 days, leaving J.J. with Charles. During this time, Charles decides to file for divorce and for temporary custody of J.J. He also changes the beneficiary of his $1 million life insurance policy from Lori to his sister, Kay Woodcock. During her absence, Lori hacks into Charles' life insurance account to add a password/pin (potentially to keep him out). Charles eventually finds out and calls the insurance company to correct the issue.

March 2019 - Charles dismisses the petition for divorce. It's unknown as to why he chooses to do so, but there was talk at the time that Charles and Lori were going to "work things out". During this time, Lori returns after abandoning Charles and J.J. for 58 days.

June 20, 2019 - Lori moves into a rental home in Chandler, Arizona.

July 11, 2019 - Charles Vallow is shot and killed by Alex Cox, one of Lori's brothers. Charles had arrived to pick up J.J. and take him to school when an altercation broke out. The story given to Chandler PD is as follows: Charles came to pick J.J. up from school. J.J. was in the car when fighting began between Charles and Lori. Things began to get physical, which caused Tylee to come out with a baseball bat to defend Lori. Tylee poked Charles with the bat a couple of times before he grabbed the bat from her. Alex stepped in and "told them they needed to separate." Lori then left with Tylee. Charles and Alex continued to argue, eventually leading Charles to hit Alex in the back of the head with the bat. Alex then went into the bedroom he had stayed in the night before to retrieve his gun. Alex claimed he told Charles to put the bat down and when he wouldn't, Alex shot Charles in the chest. About 40 minutes later, Alex called 911, claiming that the incident had "just happened." No arrests are made at this time.

July 12, 2019 - Lori sent a group text message to Charles Vallow's sons to let them know that their father had passed. The text reads,

"Hi boys. I have very sad news. Your dad passed away yesterday. I'm working on making arrangements and I'll keep you informed with what's going on. I'm still not sure how to handle things. Just want you to know that I love you and so did your dad!"

She then fails to respond to follow up messages for hours or days at a time, keeping her statements vague when she does say anything.

July 2019 - Though the exact day remains unclear, Lori calls to claim the $1 million life insurance policy on Charles shortly after his death, only to find the beneficiary had been changed. Also, on another unknown date in July, Lori and Chad Daybell begin exchanging text messages that read almost like a romance novel, even referring to themselves using the names "James" and "Elena" to describe a romantic, sexual relationship.

July 25, 2019 (approx.) - Kay Woodcock (J.J. 's grandmother) gets a text from Lori Vallow that said, "5 kids and no money and his sister gets everything."

August 10, 2019 - This is the last time Kay Woodcock hears from J.J. Vallow via FaceTime. The call was later reported to last only 35 seconds.

August 30, 2019 - Lori stops at the workplace parking lot of her eldest son, Colby, to tell him that she, Tylee, and J.J. are moving the next day.

August 31, 2019 - Lori moves with Tylee and J.J. from Chandler, AZ to Rexburg, ID.

September 8, 2019 - Rexburg Police say that Lori, Alex, J.J., and Tylee took a day trip to Yellowstone National Park. A photo taken from Lori's iCloud account on this date is the last record of Tylee being alive.

September 9, 2019 - Investigators later determine this to be the date on which Alex Cox was on Chad Daybell's property, likely burning and burying Tylee Ryan. Chad Daybell tells his wife

Tammy that he shot a raccoon and had buried it in their pet cemetery.

September 23, 2039 - J.J.is listed as an "unexcused absence" at Kennedy Elementary School. This date is later determined in June 2020 to be when Alex Cox was on Chad Daybell's property likely burying J.J. Vallow.

October 2, 2019 - Lori orders a ring on Amazon through Charles' account. The ring was silver with Malachite insets. It's the same ring that appears on Lori's hand in Chad and Lori's wedding photos.

October 3, 2019 - Browser history from the same computer used to order the ring shows searches for the terms: 'wedding dresses', 'white XL wedding clothes for men' and 'swimming trunks for men'.

October 19, 2019 - Chad Daybell's wife, Tammy, dies in her sleep at 49 years old. At the time, the original cause of death was listed as "cardiac arrest." The family does not request an autopsy.

October 22, 2019 - Tammy Daybell is buried in the Evergreen Cemetery in Springville, UT.

Late October/Early November 2019 - Chad Daybell applies for and receives $430,000 in a life insurance cash-out following his wife's death.

November 5, 2019 - Chad Daybell marries Lori Vallow, just 17 days after the death of his first wife. The wedding photos show no sign of Tylee or J.J. The photos are exclusively of Chad and Lori dancing on the beach in Hawaii.

Mid-November 2019- Chad and Lori return to Rexburg, ID from their wedding and honeymoon in Hawaii.

November 25, 2019 - Kay Woodcock hacks into Charles' email account using one of the three passwords he would always use. She discovered the Amazon purchases were sent to an address in Rexburg, ID. Using this, Kay called in a welfare check on the children.

November 26. 2019 - Rexburg Police conduct a welfare check on Tylee and J.J. Police say both Chad and Lori gave false statements concerning the whereabouts of the kids. Eventually, Lori claims that J.J. was staying with a friend in Gilbert, AZ, which later proved to be false. That same evening, Chad and Lori leave Rexburg for Hawaii again.

November 27, 2019 - Detectives show up at Colby Ryan's door asking if he has any information on J.J. or Tylee. This is the first time he learns his mom and siblings were living in Rexburg.

December 11, 2019 - Tammy Daybell's body is exhumed by the Utah Office of Medical Examiners to conduct an autopsy, as her death was now being considered suspicious. An independent investigation is initiated by the Fremont County Sheriff's Office.

December 12, 2019 - Alex Cox, 51, was found unresponsive at his home by his 25-year-old stepson, Joseph Lopez. Upon examination, Alex's death is ruled to be from natural causes, and his body is cremated soon after.

December 20, 2019 - Rexburg Police declare Tylee and J.J. missing and formally announce their investigation into the matter.

They ask for help from the public in locating the children, who have now been missing since September. Rexburg Police also identify Lori and Chad and "persons of interest."

January 25, 2020 - Lori Vallow and Chad Daybell are found in Princeville, which is located on the island of Kauai in Hawaii. Lori is issued a child protection order by the Idaho court, which demands that she physically produce Tylee and J.J. to the Idaho Department of Health and Welfare in Rexburg, ID within five days.

January 30, 2020 - The date set for Lori to produce her children for the Idaho Court comes and passes; Lori fails to appear.

February 20, 2020 - Kauai Police take Lori into custody, and she is charged with two felony counts of desertion and nonsupport of dependent children, resisting or obstructing officers, criminal solicitation to commit a crime, and contempt of court.

February 21, 2020 - Lori Vallow appears in front of a judge in Kauai, who sets Lori's bail at $5 million and orders Lori to surrender her passports. Lori's attorney requests the bail be reduced to $10,000, but this is denied by the judge. Lori is then booked into the Kauai Community Correctional Facility.

February 29, 2020 - Chad Daybell returns to Rexburg, ID.

March 5, 2020 - Lori Vallow Daybell is extradited to Rexburg, ID.

June 9, 2020 - Fremont County Sheriff Deputies, Rexburg Police officers, and FBI agents serve a search warrant for the home of Chad Daybell in Salem, ID. Chad is arrested at about midday. At 1:30 pm, a press conference is given to announce that:

Human remains had been found on the site, and

Chad Daybell had been arrested. Chad is charged with destruction and concealment of evidence.

June 11, 2020 - An autopsy summary report is released identifying the remains of J.J. Vallow, as confirmed by photographic evidence. The summary also includes verification of the remains of Tylee Ryan, which were confirmed by an orthodontist due to the state of Tylee's body.

June 13, 2020 - Law enforcement officially confirms the two bodies to be those of J.J. Vallow and Tylee Ryan based on the report given by the Medical Examiner.

June 19, 2020 - ***WARNING: This date contains graphic information concerning the remains of Tylee and J.J. If this is your first time learning about these details, please be prepared, as they may be disturbing to some readers. ***

East Idaho News reports on the sealed affidavit released by the Fremont County Seventh Judicial District:

"A patch of ground was located on the north edge of the property near a pond that appeared to be disturbed. The first layer of sod revealed several large, flat rocks. Under the rocks were some flat paneling. When removed, investigators saw a round object covered in black plastic. Once the round object had been exposed, a strong odor was noticed. An incision in the plastic revealed another layer of white plastic. Another incision was made and revealed what appeared to be the crown of a head covered in light, brown hair. The dirt around the object was carefully removed and revealed a body that was tightly wrapped in plastic and secured with duct tape.

"A second area was discovered roughly near the center of the property, close to a fire pit. During this search, the remains of a cat and dog were found. Investigators searched the soil further and discovered what appeared to be two bones. It was unclear whether or not these were human bones based on the location. However, upon further investigation into the surrounding dirt, more bones were found, as well as some tissue. Some of these bones and tissue had been charred, while others weren't. Upon discovery of these items, it was concluded that they were the remains of a non-adult human." [*]

The above events resulted in the charges eventually laid against Lori Vallow Daybell and Chad Daybell. Lori's trial took place in April 2023. At the time of writing. Chad's trial is scheduled to begin April 1, 2024.

We'd like to give a big thank you to Ken, one of our listeners, who compiled much of the information presented below. The drafted timeline he provided us with was massively helpful in putting together all these pieces of info.

[*]staff, EastIdahoNews.com. "Read: Probable Cause Details Discovery of Tylee and JJ's Bodies." East Idaho News, June 19, 2020. https://www.eastidahonews.com/2020/06/read-probable-cause-details-discovery-of-tylee-and-jjs-bodies/.

About the Authors

Adam Cox is a dad, brother, uncle, and friend. He is from Rialto California, but has lived in several states and cities over the years due to his radio career. He was a radio morning show host for several years, but has recently left the industry. He is a published author; his first book was a true story about his radio career titled "My crazy Radio Life."

He is a senior pro pickleball player and pickleball instructor. He loves all sports and has been an athlete my whole life. He recently moved to the Phoenix Arizona area to be closer to his son Zac.

He hosts a podcast with his Uncle Rex called Silver Linings.

Rex Conner has developed expertise in leading people and organizations to achieve predictable positive results by applying natural laws. His professional work has taken him inside more than fifty companies in more than two dozen industries.

In numerous keynote speeches, articles, and interviews, people have enjoyed "Train-a-saurus Rex's" new perspectives on timeless principles that exponentially enhance success in human performance.

His educational background includes an undergraduate degree, two master's degrees, and a doctorate degree. However, his credentials to write this book come more from his awareness of how natural laws govern life and from his sincere desire for you to align with those natural laws as you find what you judge to be the richness that life has to offer you.

Rex is the author of the book What if Common Sense Was Common Practice in Business? He lives in Southern Utah with his wife, Lisa. They work hard, play hard, and spend rich time with their children and grandchildren.